Museum Object Lessons for the Digital Age

I0894427

Museum Object Lessons for the Digital Age

Haidy Geismar

UCL PRESS

First published in 2018 by
UCL Press
University College London
Gower Street
London WC1E 6BT

Available to download free: www.ucl.ac.uk/ucl-press

Text © Haidy Geismar, 2018
Images © Copyright holders named in captions, 2018

Haidy Geismar has asserted her right under the Copyright, Designs and Patents Act 1988 to be identified as author of this work.

A CIP catalogue record for this book is available from The British Library.

This book is published under a Creative Commons 4.0 International license (CC BY 4.0). This license allows you to share, copy, distribute and transmit the work; to adapt the work and to make commercial use of the work providing attribution is made to the authors (but not in any way that suggests that they endorse you or your use of the work). Attribution should include the following information:

Geismar, H. 2018. *Museum Object Lessons for the Digital Age*. London: UCL Press. DOI: https://doi.org/10.14324/111.9781787352810

Further details about Creative Commons licenses are available at http://creativecommons.org/licenses/

ISBN: 978–1–78735–283–4 (Hbk.)
ISBN: 978–1–78735–282–7 (Pbk.)
ISBN: 978–1–78735–281–0 (PDF)
ISBN: 978–1–78735–284–1 (epub)
ISBN: 978–1–78735–285–8 (mobi)
ISBN: 978–1–78735–286–5 (html)
DOI: https://doi.org/10.14324/111.9781787352810

This book is dedicated to the memory of Gillian Conquest.

Acknowledgements

For feedback and friendship at different moments I am grateful to: Bruce Altshuler, Joshua Bell, Clare Harris, Aaron Glass, Hannah Knox, Daniel Miller, Katja Müller, Stephen Neale, Maia Nuku, Laura Peers, Ciraj Rassool, Antonia Walford and two anonymous reviewers for UCL Press. Thanks to Maia Nuku, Caroline Wright, Harriet Loffler, Kura Puke, Stuart Foster, Te Matahiapo Research Organization, Giancarlo Amati, Sebastian Chan, Ludovic Coupaye, Adam Drazin, Susanne Küchler and Delphine Mercier for their collaboration and conversation during the course of research and writing. The research and writing was undertaken since I started in my present position at UCL in 2012. I am grateful for the support of a research fellowship at the Bard Graduate Center in New York, Autumn 2015, and for the ongoing support from the Department of Anthropology at UCL. Special thanks to the Berlin Writers' Workshop (with intense gratitude to Jennifer Deger for all the support and feedback).

This work was also refined through opportunities to present and discuss at: Heidelberg University; Halle University Museum 4.0 lecture series; Aarhus University's Precious Relics Workshop; the Museum Studies and Anthropology Seminar at Johns Hopkins, Baltimore, USA; the research seminar at Bard Graduate Center, New York; the Austronesian Seminar, LSE; the Museums at the Cross Roads Symposium at the Mathers Museum, Indiana University; the Transforming Data Workshop, CRESC-Open University; the Visual, Material and Museum Anthropology Seminar at the University of Oxford; the London Historical Geographers Seminar, Senate House; and the Centre for Anthropological Research on Museums and Heritage at Humboldt University, Berlin. Thanks to Nora Al-Badri and Jan Nikolai Nelles for their permission to use the image of Nefertiti on the cover.

Thanks to Chris Penfold, Jaimee Biggins and the editorial team at UCL Press.

*Please note: all referenced web pages have been archived through the Wayback Machine and so can be accessed, either live or dead, through https://archive.org/web/.

Contents

List of figures

Introduction

'Object Lesson: An example from real life that teaches a lesson or explains something.'[1]

This book explores the interface of digital and analogue media within museum practices and technologies of exhibition, classification, archiving and collection. It is an invitation to think about digital in historical and material context, and to meditate upon how collections are made, and remade, over and over again. The term 'object lesson' means more than simply using artefacts for teaching purposes. Rather, object lessons are arguments about the world made through things. They are educational, performative and fundamentally material. As Lorraine Daston describes, object lessons are ideas brought into being by things, not just as communicating vehicles, but as sites of meaning *animated* by their materiality.[2]

Museums are the perfect sites for the production and dissemination of object lessons. They are curated spaces, often curiously set apart from our everyday lives, in which we, the public, are invited to learn very particular things about the world. The neo-classical sculpture hall, the white cube contemporary art space and the reconstructed period room have become sites of learning within which visitors may lose themselves in the text of labels and display panels, the narratives of audio guides and guided tours. The power of these spaces is evident in the global surge of museum-building projects: nation-states, corporations and local communities are investing more and more in spaces to collect, curate and exhibit their histories, narratives and identities.[3] Object lessons constitute powerful subjectivities in museums – for instance, forging experience and understandings of 'the public', 'participation' and 'citizenship'.[4] In all of these museum projects, object lessons emerge in the ways in which collections are placed together, framed, strategically narrated, contextualised in architecture, and in language, and sensuously experienced in order to generate a vision of 'real life': the material generation of a view

Figure 1 Blind children studying the globe. Photograph by Julius Kirschner, 1914, © American Museum of Natural History, Image: 335068. Reproduced with permission.

of the world that we can believe as true.[5] Object lessons are therefore both ontological (they tell us something about what there is) and epistemological (they help us interpret and explain what there is).

And yet, the relationships between collections and displays in museums, and notions of real life have to be carefully constructed within the period rooms of decorative arts museums, the halls of 'Africa, Oceania and the Americas', in stores and archives, in the community curated gallery, and in the overcrowded shelves of the teaching collection. Here, 'real life' is created inside the collection through technologies and techniques of display as much as it is by the materiality of the artefacts. In these spaces, which are prone to wear and tear, dust and disintegration, digital technologies are often experienced as shiny and new, without precedent, layering new forms of interpretation and experience onto historical collections.[6] As I will show here, as much as digital media brings new ways of looking at and understanding collections, it also re-presents, and refracts, earlier representational techniques. Holograms, virtual reality and interactive touch screens continue the reality effects, and object lessons, of model-making, dioramas and period rooms. These are all technologies that purport to capture the outside world and bring it into the space of the museum, and they all also produce new ways of being in, and learning about, the world.

It is quite common to imagine the digital as immaterial – as a set of experiences or form of information sequestered somewhere 'in the cloud'. To counter this there is a vibrant emerging literature focused on the material infrastructures that underpin digital networks and which enable digital media to circulate and pulsate its way around the world – from the electrical grid to server farms and undersea cables.[7] New academic fields such as Platform Studies and Format Theory aim to ground ephemeral philosophies of the digital by paying careful attention to the socio-political, historical and material forms that structure digital media.[8] This book aims to do the same for our understanding of digital museum objects – to fill the lacunae that imagines digital objects as fundamentally immaterial and to explore more fully what kind of objects, and collections, they are. The definition of a digital object slips between digital files that themselves serve as their own kind of 'objects' and the technologies (screens, phones, kiosks) that deliver them. The continual slippage in definition around digital objecthood helps us to recognise that what Daston describes as 'common sense thing-ontology … chunky and discrete' does not generally extend to the digital in museums. We often have trouble describing the digital using the language of museum collections, focusing more on concepts such as knowledge, networks and media.[9] By proposing a reorientation of our awareness of digital media in museums, I argue here that we need to think about the digital not only as material, rather than immaterial, but also in terms of a trajectory of materiality that links our commonplace understandings of the digital to the analogue, information to material, systems to structures, knowledge to form.[10] Object lessons – the deliberate harnessing of the material world to create knowledge – bring materiality and knowledge together into many different forms. In fact, as I shall present here, imagining the digital/analogue as a divide (rather than a continuum) is not a particularly productive way of understanding the particular materiality, and historicity, of digital practices and objects in museums.

Many people understand digital technologies – particularly those that produce the expansive internet, sometimes referred to as Web 2.0 or more recently as the semantic web – as extending the civic capacities of museums, opening access, democratising curatorial authority and destabilising values of authenticity and the aura of singular artefacts. The digital components of contemporary museum practices are often presented as radical alternatives to the historical form of the museum itself, provoking a powerful sense of undoing the heavy stasis of the museum artefact with a new kind of materiality, a digital poetics that can be used to unpack the politics of museum collections.[11] This, I believe, is only half the story. In this series of chapters, each taking a single object as a starting point, I work to make sense of digital collections as objects in their own right, and locate them within the object lessons that predate the ubiquity of digital technologies within our cultural lives. In so doing I undo many of our assumptions about the nature of the digital. This is not a reactionary argument against the new, or against the digital, but rather an exhortation to take the digital seriously in more than just its own terms – to unpack the assumptions and perspectives that are built into digital museum projects.

The contemporary object lessons I explore here inhabit a 'contact zone', where old museum collections and new technologies come together, tracing the translation and extension of collections from card catalogues, storerooms and display cases into digital websites, imaging platforms and collection management systems. James Clifford's influential rendition of Mary Louise Pratt's notion of contact zones in the context of museums defines contact zones as spaces where multiple communities are drawn together, within unequal power relations, around collections.[12] The contact zone highlights the politics that draw knowledge and meaning from collections through representational practices of classification and recognition. Here, I extend the notion of the contact zone and pose a challenge to the epistemological framework we use to define the digital by exploring how the representational politics of the contact zone may be understood as a continual process of remediation. As collections extend into digital form – books, images and paper archives migrate into databases and relationships are refigured as digital social networks – the stakes are high. What is the value of older collections, shut in expensive unwieldy storage, locked into exhibitions that are out of date before they open, trapped in often troubled, colonial histories? Equally, how do we deal with the problems raised by new digital collections? How do we approach problems of promiscuous circulation, expensive infrastructures, the liability of obsolescence, dependency on technical expertise, and the capacity to engage audiences comprised of digitally literate consumers at the possible expense of others, often understood to be on the wrong side of the so-called 'digital divide'?

These obvious questions – of infrastructure, accessibility and skill – mask some even more fundamental questions about the ways in which digital objects produce knowledge and meaning both *in* and *of* the world. I write at a time when the celebratory capacities of digital technologies seem to be unlocking the museum in unprecedented ways. As you will read about in the chapters that follow, websites can make entire collections available across the world in an instant, robots can allow so-called source communities to curate collections from afar and 3D-printing technologies permit us to recreate objects destroyed by war and extremism. These projects seem to highlight how digital media are the future form of collections, and indeed of museums. More broadly, our cultural world is increasingly interacting with the 'internet of things', smart technologies and big data. The digital has become a core medium of cultural production, from the co-option of broadcast media by social media through to the dependence on cultural expression on digital platforms. Lev Manovich has described this as 'software taking command'.[13] However, one of the key lessons of museum anthropology and museum studies as academic disciplines is the deceptively simple point that museums are sites that produce as well as represent knowledge about the world.[14] We need to ask what kind of world the digital produces and how different it really is from the world that existed before. What tools do we have for understanding and appreciating the digital in a context beyond that of its own making? What kind of collection will these digital projects become? What kinds of object lesson do digital technologies, media and practices provide?

The chapters that follow each start with a specific object. They represent a personal exploration of contemporary museum object lessons that trace my own trajectory as a curator, researcher and museum visitor. I suggest that this approach reflects a broader way in which knowledge is built up in museums by their visitors, who create their own connections, while simultaneously following established narratives and curated pathways.[15] My own work over many years as a scholar and curator demonstrates both the serendipity and happenstance, the discipline and dialogue, that occur as we move around objects in museums, from collections, archives and storage into exhibition halls, websites and other digital projects. My role as a researcher, teacher and curator working with some very unique collections has allowed for a certain amount of audacity and experimentation in both the creation of new kind of object lessons and in the intervention into old ones. These personal pathways demonstrate how object lessons emerge at the interstices between the personal, the idiosyncratic, the biographical, the political and the governmental. Two chapters focus on objects housed within the collection to which I have privileged access as curator: the UCL Ethnography Collections. One chapter draws on my experiences as a visiting researcher at the Metropolitan Museum of Art, while one chapter draws on my experiences as a visitor to the Cooper Hewitt, Smithsonian Design Museum. In choosing these objects I have tried to draw upon many of the subject positions that collections gather together: visitor, artist, researcher, student, curator, stakeholder. The objects I reference are housed in New York and London, but they are situated within networks of production and exchange that extend from the South Pacific to Europe and North America, and through the World Wide Web's technological networks and infrastructures of both hardware and software. Each of these chapters traces these transformations, interconnections and remediations, emerging from a complex global web of connections, collaborations and conversations.

The objects I explore here fall into two broad categories: first, those that belong to the classic ethnographic collection (an effigy and a cloak); and second, those that seem to belong more to the technology of collections (a box and a pen). However, these categories dissolve as quickly as I can type the words to describe them on my computer, for objects are transformed into 'ethnographic collections' through the powerful exercising of museum technologies, and the tools used to do this are rendered cultural as they become entangled in the social worlds of meaning-making that characterises human engagement with objects. With my first object, a box, I describe a collaboration with artist Caroline Wright that explores the consolidation of knowledge and meaning in the form of specific artefacts. Working with deaccessioned objects, Wright asks whether value – and knowledge – is moveable, situated around the object, or located within the object. By decomposing objects into drawings and into their 'base' materials, her project raises important questions about mimesis and replication that are vital to our understanding of how the digital remediates collections.

My second object is the opposite of the wooden box: a digital device, a pen, that has become an integral part of the visitor experience of the newly reopened Cooper Hewitt, Smithsonian Design Museum in New York. The pen is a tool that aims to connect the visitor to the digitised museum catalogue. By exploring how this animates a particular perspective on design, it becomes clear that this new digital tool continues a trajectory that was established by the creation of the decorative arts as a particular museum and collecting genre in the nineteenth century. The relationality of digital databases is prefigured in the decorative arts collection, which creates image-based connections across different materials and media, allowing for their remediation through a broad process of design.

My third object continues the discussion about how artefacts make meanings by exploring multiple understandings of a Rambaramp funeral effigy from Vanuatu in the collections of the Metropolitan Museum of Art. This chapter asks how artefacts might embody multiple perspectives and draw together contradictory provenances. I explore how existing knowledge systems may, or may not, be represented digitally and expose a dominant perspective of many museum digital imaging projects that efface rather than uphold the capacity of digital media to represent, or even encode, multiplicity.

My fourth object is a Māori cloak, also in the UCL Ethnography Collections. This beautiful cloak, *Tukutuku Roimata*, has drawn together artists and interaction designers, museum professionals, anthropologists and Māori communities in London and Aotearoa New Zealand. The cloak's mediation, through both imaging technologies and social media, prompted a conversation about how digital technologies might be understood within different cultural registers and challenged us to unpack our assumptions about virtual replication using Māori notions of *wairua*, or spiritual energy.

Taken together, these chapters explore the object lessons that are produced within museum processes of digitisation. The border zone of translation, or remediation, between our understandings of old and new collections draws our attention to the interdependence of object lessons (creating knowledge from the real world) and reality effects (the use of objects to mimetically create an understanding of the real). The moment when one kind of technological mediation gives way to another is also the moment in which we learn about what we consider to be 'natural' (or real) and what we perceive to be 'socially' constructed. As collections themselves shift across platforms, what counts as a real object, worthy of preservation and care, subject to property regimes and the call of sovereignty, is also drawn into question. Moments of remediation are more than just processes of translation – they are moments in which knowledge and meaning itself are produced. Here, I work hard to counter the perception of indexicality that increasingly accompanies digital museum objects – the perception that digital reproductions are somehow *more real* than other representational technologies, that social networks within digital space are somehow more social and more networked than those previously facilitated by the museum. Rather, I explore how understandings of the social, of the ways in which the digital shapes our embodied encounters with collections, and of the ways in which the digital itself is emerging as a knowledge system, can at times be curiously reactionary as well as opening up conversations in truly novel and exciting directions.[16]

1
Ways of knowing

Object lessons in museums present contemporary meanings and narratives around collections but also highlight the processes through which knowledge is constructed. The history of museums tends to be presented in a linear narrative in which collections are ordered through increasingly systematic classification, at the same time becoming more public. There is a standard history of museums that progresses from the Greek temples of the muses (*museion*) through European cabinets of curiosities into royal and aristocratic collections that, through social upheaval and colonial expansion, evolved into the civic and national institutions that benchmark our contemporary museum landscape.[1]

Yet this teleological perspective, in which disorder gives way to order, chaos to rationality, polyphony to stable meaning, and private to public, is continually confounded by the same sets of objects used to constitute it. Running parallel to the institutional collecting of great families and royal societies come the idiosyncratic collections of missionaries, mercenaries, doctors and local enthusiasts.[2] Supposedly rational and systematic scholarly collections contain objects bought with emotional or obsessive impulses, or objects that were stolen or looted.[3] Within collections founded to display the best of human society and the natural world, we find exhibitions designed to illustrate our understandings of abnormality, transgression and immorality.[4] Alongside collections designed to educate and edify we find others intended to confound and confuse.[5] As Stephen Greenblatt has described, almost all collections provoke both resonance ('the power of the object to reach out beyond its formal boundaries to a larger world') *and* wonder ('the power of the displayed objects … to convey an arresting sense of uniqueness') as parallel ways of experiencing and learning about the world.[6]

While a compelling genealogy of contemporary museum practices and interests could be drawn by looking back to the Early Modern period or even further back to the Classical age, the Victorian-era museum that emerged from the intensive collecting enabled by European Imperial expansion, legitimating the colonial nation and modelling citizenship across the divides of both race and class along the way, is often presented as the apotheosis of this history. The Victorian Era is often seen as playing a critical role in both defining the modern museum and purifying the object lessons it offers into a series of visually mediated didactic experiences.[7] Nineteenth-century object lessons, emerging within newly established museums of science, industry and ethnography, in world fairs and within new local art museums and historical societies, were dedicated explorations of progress, innovation, national and colonial sovereignties.[8] The legacy of the nineteenth-century object lesson continues to inflect our understanding of how museums 'work' today. Discussions about the right of museums to 'own' culture, to speak on behalf of people and their culture(s) and to represent others often start with the nineteenth century. For it was during this time that the legacies of imperialism, colonialism and class hegemonies, the normative standards for citizenship and consumer identities were consolidated across the (museum) world.[9]

I start my exploration of these issues in the Pitt Rivers Museum in Oxford because it was one of the first places in which anthropologists used ethnographic collections to develop the notion of the object lesson. The Pitt Rivers Museum, founded in 1884, is famous for perpetuating in many of its cases the original framing and theorisation of its founder, Augustus Henry Lane Fox (General Pitt Rivers), who built up models of social evolution through the typological comparison of collections. In his 1881 presidential address to the Anthropological Institute, Oxford professor E.B. Tylor described the museum being proposed by General Pitt Rivers as 'not so much a collection as a set of object-lessons in the development of culture'.[10] For Tylor and Pitt Rivers, museum collections were the perfect fusion of object and idea. In the case of the Pitt Rivers Museum, the ideas were about the evolution of human culture, and by extension human races, across the globe. Within its cases, even today, hundreds of years of human history are compressed into an object lesson of Darwinian-inflected cultural progression from primitive to modern, allowing us to imagine the world from the point of view of a Victorian collector living in Oxford.[11] This series of object lessons has been confounded over the years by the sheer scale of the collection and the visual romance of the museum's crowded display cases. Moving far beyond the convergence of social evolution and typological display, the museum has also become the home of new museum anthropologies that use the sheer

Figure 2 View of the central hall of the Pitt Rivers Museum as it was in 2015. Photograph by Haidy Geismar. Reproduced with permission of the Pitt Rivers Museum.

density of displayed objects to think critically about the challenging past and present of the collections.[12]

At first glance, the Pitt Rivers can be seen to teach today's visitor (at least) two kinds of object lessons. One is about the rationales of nineteenth-century ethnology and the ways in which those at the time understood cultural differences in object form. The other is suggestive

Figure 3 'Kwakwaka'wakw Indians of Vancouver Island', Hall of Northwest Coast Indians, American Museum of Natural History, installation view from 1916, image 34995. © American Museum of Natural History. Reproduced with permission.

of a contemporary, sensuous and collaborative visitor experience, summarised by the poet James Fenton, who looks at the exhibit hall and is filled with nostalgia:

> *Outdated*
> *though the cultural anthropological system be*
> *The lonely and unpopular*
> *Might find the landscape of their childhood marked out*
> *Here, in the chaotic piles of souvenirs.*[13]

A second starting point for this book is the Hall of Northwest Coast Indians at the American Museum of Natural History in New York which was formally opened in 1899. Like the Pitt Rivers, the Hall both evokes an earlier era of museum anthropology and continues to excite both critical and nostalgic responses from visitors making apparent the tensions between the complex history of anthropological theories of race and culture and the sensuous powers of display. The life groups created by Franz Boas, some of which are still on display, demonstrate how, by

Figure 4 'Kwakwa̱ka̱'wakw Indians of Vancouver Island', as seen on display in 2016, in the Hall of Northwest Coast Indians, © American Museum of Natural History. Reproduced with permission.

1906, technologies of display were explicitly working against the evolutionary theories of mainstream anthropology. This technological transference from typological and evolutionary display to life groups did not *only* import new ways of objectifying living peoples in the museum, freezing culture into anthropological categories and types. It is also an example of how scholar-curators such as Boas were trying to work against the freezing of time in the natural history collection, and its evolutionary underpinnings, by presenting native peoples in the context of their own (albeit idealised) life experiences.[14] As complex object lessons about the 'real world', these groups presented a series of new arguments about cultural differences, and about the contemporaneity of diverse human experiences.[15]

Alison Griffiths has discussed the spectacular techniques that created reality effects through dioramas, life groups and other immersive technologies in the nineteenth-century museum, highlighting their dual purpose of provoking 'shivers down the spine' as well as informational and didactic experiences.[16] Boas' curation of the hall presented tableaus of people engaged in everyday activities, and the later curation by his successor, Clark Wissler, invited the visitor to travel up and down through the 'Culture Areas' of the Northwest Pacific Coast as they moved across the gallery. Today we read these life groups as relics of a former museology – freezing native peoples in timeless tradition as they were being systematically moved off their tribal lands, disenfranchised and, worse, systematically killed in a series of violent conflicts over land and sovereignty.[17]

As the growing focus on consultation, collaboration and co-production in museums exemplifies, it is however remiss to understand engagements with museum collections only through the lens of exhibitions and solely through the lens of the visual encounter. Within all museums there are many hidden histories, predicated on the sensuous intimacies that come from touching and using collections outside of the display cases, in places such as the archive, storeroom or even outside the museum's walls. Many of these initial engagements used to be the privileged domain of the curator and scholar before collections were opened up to other stakeholders. For instance, as I discuss below, Boas used his own body as a reference point for the life groups of Northwest Coast Indians he produced for the Columbian Exposition and they therefore reflect his engagements as a fieldworker as well as a museum practitioner (see Figure 9). At the Pitt Rivers Museum, Oxford students experimented with the throwing sticks and boomerangs sent to the museum from Australia (see Figure 5).[18] In Cambridge, anthropologists dressed up, on occasion, in the Museum of Archaeology and Anthropology collections at garden parties (see Figure 6). All of these uses highlight the interpretive domination of collections through an intimate domestication of artefacts by curators, collectors and anthropologists.

While some of these engagements are more frivolous than others, and they all indicate ongoing and embodied hierarchies of authority over cultural collections, I draw on them here to propose an alternative set of object lessons to the ones presented within glass display cases, with a view that this will help us to better understand the resonance of digital objects and the lessons they provide. The intimacy of touch, smell and other kinds of sensuous engagement with things provides another way into collections to the usual focus on text and visual narrative as read from the contents of glass display cases. The dominant emphasis in museum studies on spectacular appreciation belies other modes of engagement with collections and other kinds of object lessons.[19] These modes may be historically less documented, but they are no less powerful. They may be found within the sensuous intimacy of corporeal engagement with collections, drawing on senses such as touch, and registers such as storytelling, smudging, eating and singing.[20] Together, the full sensorium of engagement with collections pushes us to understand museum object lessons as powerful forms of material mimesis, in which knowledge is

Figure 5 Group portrait of Francis Howe Seymour Knowles, Henry Balfour (examiner), Barbara Freire-Marreco, James Arthur Harley, 1908. Photographer unknown (possibly Alfred Robinson), 1998.266.3. © Pitt Rivers Museum, University of Oxford. Reproduced with permission.

Figure 6 Professor John Hutton's retirement party at The Orchard, Grantchester, with members of the Faculty of Archaeology and Anthropology dressed in museum artefacts, c. 1950. Professor Hutton wearing a hat and garland, Reo Fortune in the middle and another person dressed as a Plains Indian. P.100613. © Cambridge University Museum of Archaeology and Anthropology. Reproduced with permission.

constructed not just within exhibitions but by bodily connections to the collections. Such sensuous connection formed part of a new museology that emerged in the 1980s and 1990s to re-situate museums as sites of cultural production as well as cultural representation, with everyday visitors, rather than scholars, at their core.[21]

From the vantage point of my present, as I write in 2017, the nineteenth-century object lesson is often used to present historic collections as a 'problem' that new forms of social and political engagement, implemented with new technologies, can solve. As all the projects I discuss here demonstrate, these histories continue to mark the present in ways that need to be both understood and remembered. Screens both replicate the boundaries of glass cases and enable new kinds of visitor experience; social media both enables existing source communities and creates new stakeholders. As we shall see throughout this volume, the use of digital media in museums provokes numerous contradictory discourses. It emerges as a frame for discussions that lament the end of social relations as well as those that celebrate the constitution of a new public sphere.[22] Digital media are seen to embody both the poetics and politics of resistance as well as new intensifications of government surveillance and control.[23] Digital objects are used to teach us about inattention and distraction as well as providing new, more inclusive, learning experiences. They are often used explicitly as object lessons to discuss both immateriality and to materialise global networks and infrastructures.[24] Many of these polarising object lessons are just as moralising, and as beset with cultural assumptions as were the Victorian object lessons in the earliest ethnographic displays. By presenting digital media and technologies as either firmly utopian, or despairingly dystopian, arguments are made about the power of the digital to structure many aspects of our life, in much the same way that Victorians imagined the museum as a technology of social arrangement and example.[25]

Within museums, the presence of digital media is often presented as a utopian alternative to older museum practices, bringing 'new' flexibility, accessibility and openness to the weighty solidity of 'old' collections. For example, some have come to celebrate the potentials of 'virtual' or digital repatriation, the accessibility of crowd-curated exhibitions and the democratisation of the folksonomy as powerful alternatives to the authoritative classifications and exhibitionary tactics used by curators and other experts in museums.[26] In many museums, media labs have become increasingly institutionalised as spaces that use digital technologies, and develop partnerships between digital designers and museums, in order to illuminate some of the key aspirations and object lessons of the collections. In so doing, very specific expectations about the capacities and nature of digital technologies are imported into the museum space. These digital experiences are the publicly visible sites of private labs in which visitor experience, data and digital design are put together in experimental ways. For instance, the Media Lab at the Metropolitan Museum of Art is tucked away in a section of the museum that is inaccessible to the public, part of the Digital Media department. When Thomas Campbell resigned as director in 2017 in the wake of a number of financial controversies at the museum, many staff of the Media Lab lost their jobs. This experimental space, a zone that exists alongside the traditional departments of the museum, is currently being rethought. The Media Lab has hosted a number of experimental projects around the museum; for example, printing and casting objects in edible sugar, mashing 3D scans to print hybrid objects, or projecting colour images onto the Temple of

Dendur in order to present research into its original pigments.[27] These projects exemplify a particular kind of celebration of the capacities of digital technologies to not only remediate but also refigure collections – a refiguration that is often seen as an endpoint in itself rather than as a pathway back to the original collection.

It is here, gazing at a 3D print of hybrid object made by fusing together two classical sculptures in the collections of the Metropolitan Museum of Art, that I begin my enquiry into what object lessons are emerging in the museums of the twenty-first century. How do digital practices engage with pre-existing museum practices of collecting, curating, conserving and exhibiting? What new communities and skills are being brought into the museum? What exclusions are extended and maintained? How do digital technologies allow us to open up the received history of object lessons in museums and how can they challenge our assumptions about the relationship between material form and knowledge, objects and information, meaning and matter?

Figure 7 Screengrab of a 3D print of Leda and the Marsyas by Jon Monaghan, published on Thingiverse, 2 June 2012. https://www.thingiverse.com/thing:24064. Reproduced under a CC license.

2
Digital object lessons and their precursors

The fundamental argument of this book is that we need to pay attention to the specific contexts, as well as materialities, of digital objects and that digital media in museums exist in a long-standing continuum or process of mediation, technological mimesis and objectification. In an exchange of comment in the journal *Science*, Franz Boas argued with his colleague O.T. Mason about the purpose and nature of museum collections.[1] The debate emerged from the growing museological tension between the spectacular nature of individual objects and their contextualisation within academic and scientific knowledge systems. Boas, summarising his position later, noted:

> *I think no word has ever been said that is less true than Dr. Brown Goode's oft-repeated statement that a museum is a well-arranged collection of labels illustrated by specimens. On the contrary, the attraction for the public is the striking specimen; and whatever additional information either the label or the surrounding specimens may be able to convey to the mind of the visitor is the only result that can be hoped for.*[2]

Boasian museology started with the spectacular – an object or life group – and moved from there to the labels, the expedition report (on display in the gallery) and, for the truly dedicated visitor, the resource of the museum library. Boas abandoned the museum shortly after these debates, in large part because he perceived his experiments with display to have failed to displace some of the prevailing evolutionary theories of race and culture with which he vehemently disagreed. His creation of life models and groups, and the layering of different kinds of information around objects, did not succeed in animating objects and allowing visitors to understand them in context. Rather, it created a new, museological context for the collection, whose existential and dusty historicity was at odds with the dynamic fluidity of the cultural processes that he was attempting to present. At the same time, Boas was unaware of some of the implicit narratives his own theory of culture presented in the form of life groups and cultural areas. In undermining social evolutionary understandings of progress and arguments about racial determinism, Boas' dynamic life groups themselves became frozen in time. They presented multiple layers of information – from single object, to tableau, to label, to voluminous text – resulting in the dissolution of the object into an informational domain ignoring or neglecting the ways in which objects could also be seen as compressions of information about collectors and museums as well as their original producers. What kind of a lesson is this for the digital age?

Some of the interpretive problems in moving from objects to anthropological theory are in certain respects built into the very notion of permanent exhibitions, especially for ethnographic collections that aim to present living peoples and which will by definition

Figure 8 *Windows on the Collection,* at the National Museum of the American Indian, Smithsonian Institute, Washington D.C., 2005. Photograph by Gwyneria Isaac. Reproduced with permission.

be permanently trapped in a present moment that will always be out of date. Film, photography and now digital media have long been used to inject a sense of contemporaneity into this temporal vortex. It is, however, important to unpack how text, images and objects work together to create reality effects. Digital media has the tendency to compress multiple forms of information into a single space, usually apprehended through a screen. Gwyneira Isaac, curator of North American Ethnology at the Smithsonian National Museum of Natural History, has written about the touch-screen displays that give access to collections held within the National Museum of the American Indian (NMAI). She argues that the touch screens themselves have become 'the objects'. Rather than adding layers of contextual information to the other displays, the interactive screens scattered throughout the displays have themselves become primary objects as vitrines that curate and exhibit the collections. Isaac suggests that these digital screens have become not just the vehicle for delivering information but objects of appreciation in their own right that mimetically appropriate the effects and engagements of glass cases.[3] In this way it could be argued that the NMAI took the legacy of George Gustav Heye – one of the most prolific collectors of Native American material culture – and extended his reach into digital space, converting an abundance of objects behind glass into an abundance of digital images on screens.[4]

The questions that were raised in nineteenth-century museum debates about the relation between the singular artefact and more general kinds of knowledge and information have returned full force at the turn of the twenty-first century, inflecting our understanding of the digital domain and the questions we often ask about whether the 'virtual' is 'real'.[5] The issues, and object lessons, raised are simultaneously epistemological, experiential and political. Drawing on material culture studies we can understand any object as a material, social, political and epistemological palimpsest.[6] Analysing digital objects in this way can help us to better understand the capacities of digital media to participate in the mimetic and constructed process of producing arguments about the real world inside the museum.

Boas' life groups were active demonstrations of how an embodied experience of objects is literally built into museum object lessons. Boas himself was one of the models for the famous Hamat'sa life group displayed at the Atlanta World's Fair in 1895, which went on to become a permanent display at the United States National Museum of Natural History.[7] The Hamat'sa life group, produced from photographs of Boas modelling the ritual as he observed and documented it, was replicated in

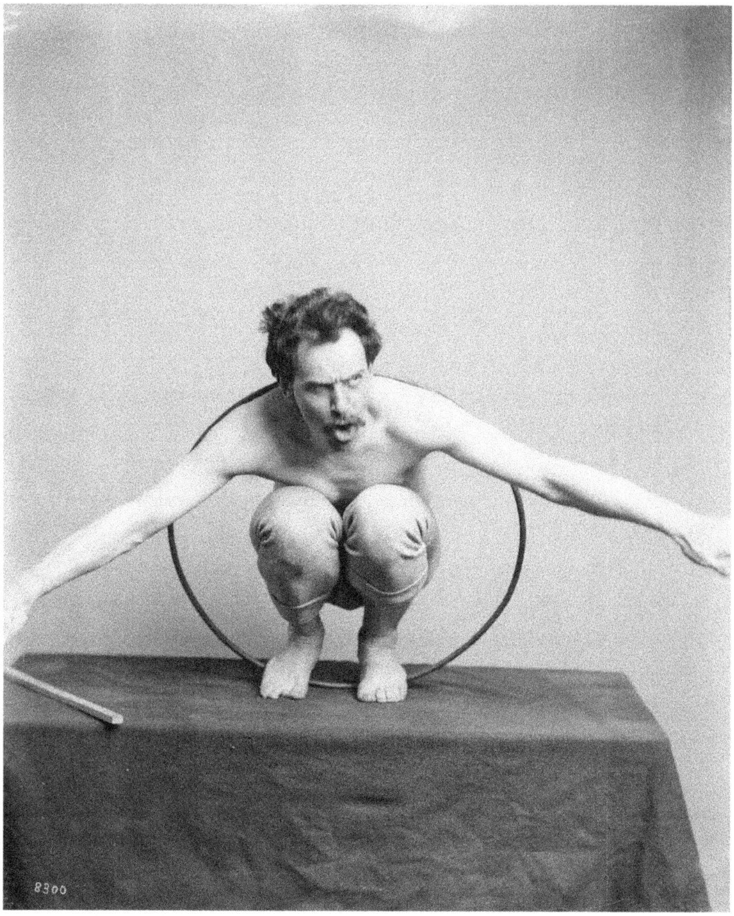

Figure 9 Franz Boas posing for figure in United States National Museum exhibit entitled 'Hamat'sa coming out of secret room', 1895 or before, photographer unknown. Negative MNH 8300, National Anthropological Archives. © Smithsonian Institution. Reproduced with permission.

1904 at the Chicago Field Museum, and in 1927 at the Milwaukee Public Museum, and also appears on the cover of George Stocking's seminal volume about museum anthropology, *Objects and Others*.[8] As an object lesson, this installation demonstrates how knowledge is generated not just by spectatorship and visual circulation but through forms of corporeal mimesis that are projected onto and implicate the viewer through imaging technologies of both photography and model-making. It enables visitors to understand the Hamat'sa from inside the display by imagining their own capacity to inhabit the position of the Hamat'sa dancers while also being spectators at the ceremony, and in the museum.

Figure 10 United States National Museum exhibit display case prepared by Franz Boas: 'Hamat'sa Coming out of Secret Room', 1895. NAA INV 09070600, National Anthropological Archives. © Smithsonian Institution. Reproduced with permission.

As Alison Griffiths has argued in relation to a number of compelling examples, from planetaria to IMAX cinemas, bodily connections are implicit within museum imaging technologies and are therefore built into the exhibition experience and technologies of spectatorship. This bodily perspective allows us to relocate our preoccupation with the visual in museums, and in relation to digital culture, in a more complex sensuous and experiential domain.[9] The visual experience has dominated our discussion of object lessons – for instance, in Tony Bennett's influential description of the ways in which museums exerted governmental power through the 'exhibitionary complex'.[10] Yet the power of looking, and of being looked at, exerted by the curators of museum exhibitions, is only one way in which collections can be co-opted into object lessons. If we shift our attention away from exhibitions to other museum practices of collecting, classifying, storing, conserving, researching and collaborating with communities, we see a host of other experiences in which meaning around objects is negotiated. Clifford's 'contact zone' is useful to suggest an uneven space of (colonial) encounter that increasingly gives meaning to museum collections through the engagement, in the museum, of stakeholders and communities.[11] Seeing exhibitions, and many other activities and experiences within the museum, as contact zones allows us to think about the multiplicity of experience; the varied forms of sociality; and the negotiation of authority that continually takes place around museum collections. Yet the contact zone also suggests a need to think beyond what can be seen evoking a sensorium of contact. There have been a number of important critiques of the ways in which the idea of the contact zone has been disconnected from its original usage as a space of unequal colonial relationality and used instead to redeem the problematic legacy of colonial collections. Robin Boast describes the contemporary museum contact zone as 'neo-colonial', perpetuating existing power relations within a new language of collaboration and consultation. Similarly, Nancy Marie Mithlo describes the contact zone as a 'red man's burden', shifting the responsibility of participation onto Indigenous people without changing the conditions that structure museological contact.[12] It is vital to reclaim the notion of the contact zone as not just a space of social encounter but as a political domain in which historical relationships are enacted through physical engagement between people and connections, body with wood and stone; stories and storerooms.

Figure 11 Dr Ludovic Coupaye, Jo Walsh and Rosanna Raymond of Ngāti Rānana (the London Māori Club) in the UCL Ethnography Collections, 25 January 2013. Photograph by Haidy Geismar. Reproduced with permission of all pictured.

In its fullest sense, as a way to explore power, politics, relationships and physical points of connection, the contact zone is a productive way to understand our relationship to museum collections, and can help us to figure out the entanglement of social and material contexts. In Figure 11 you can see one of my colleagues, Ludovic Coupaye, welcoming representatives of Ngāti Rānana, the London Māori Club, into the storeroom of the UCL Ethnography Collections, in order to celebrate the return of a Māori *poutokomanawa*, or carved ancestor figure, to Bloomsbury after having been on display in an exhibition at the Horniman Museum in South London. You can see Rosanna Raymond, a New Zealander of Pacific Island descent, an artist and performer and an important interlocutor for Pacific collections in London, and Jo Walsh, representing Ngāti Rānana, reading out a poem to thank the figure for his work in the exhibition and to lay him to rest for a while at UCL. You can also see the feather earrings that Raymond made for the *poutokomanawa*, which are now a permanent part of the object.[13] Taking a step back from the overpowering influence of the 'exhibitionary complex' as an interpretive framework for understanding museum materialities, the concept of the contact zone encourages us to think about how information is encoded in objects in other ways: in an experiential domain, within social spaces as well as zones of political encounter.

The interpretive tensions that arise when exploring collections require us to think carefully about where information resides and how knowledge is generated. The digital domain provokes a similar interpretive slippage to any other form of material culture:[14] do we look through digital media to the worlds that it contains and represents, or do we zoom both in and out to examine the platforms and the material affordances of the technologies themselves in structuring these worlds? And like museum collections, digital media in its broadest sense polarises the ways in which we think about the process and practice of interpretation and the mediation of social and political worlds. For every digital utopianist who celebrates the capacity of digital technologies to liberate us from past inequalities of access to knowledge, forging new communities unstratified by class, race or gender, there is a digital dystopianist who emphasises the entanglement of corporate projects of monetisation and state projects of surveillance now reaching into our most intimate moments.[15] We know that digital infrastructures perpetuate existing inequalities of access and ownership as much as they disrupt them, and that for every grand project to digitise the world's books there are at least a million images of cats.

Where, then, do digital museum collections fit into this continual back-and-forth movement between categories of object and information or knowledge and the continued relocation of material forms within other representational technologies, particularly the visual? Digital objects are often described as being pure information, floating somehow in immaterial space. At the same time, their materiality is in fact continually shifting as electrical circuits pass through cables, into hardware, through the interfaces of code and, at the moment, primarily onto screens. As Hui comments, digital materiality has its own sets of material constraints and affects:

> *Digital objects appear to human users as colourful and visible beings. At the level of programming they are text files; further down the operating system they are binary codes; finally, at the level of circuit boards they are nothing but signals generated by the values of voltage and the operation of logic gates. How, then, can we think about the voltage differences as being the substance of a digital object? Searching downward we may end up with the mediation of silicon and metal. And finally we could go into particles and fields. But this kind of reductionism doesn't tell us much about the world.*[16]

It might be helpful to see digital materiality as 'an unfolding process', not simply as an end product or a finished object.[17] Yet, despite this complexity, we generally apprehend digital museum collections via screens, which constrain and define our experience of them as objects. Despite the capacity of digital technologies to be experienced through multiple senses, and to be understood as complicated material connectors linking hardware and software often across global networks, a visual image is by far the most prominent mode in which we experience digital collections, a trajectory that links the screens of computers and mobile devices to the glass cases of a conventional museum display.

The object lessons I have been discussing so far raise a series of questions about the politics of access, and the tension between the visual or other senses as the primary museum experience. Museum object lessons also provide an interpretive shift back and forth – from understanding objects in terms of materials or culture, from the singular to the collection, from the collection to the institution, and from the collection to the world. Thinking about digital within these terms allows us to make sense of both the resonance and wonder of digital mediation.

There are a series of ideas about the digital that emerge from our engagement with digital technologies and which resonate with pre-existing object lessons in museums to produce what we might understand as a series of digital object lessons. For instance, a dominant idea about the digital is the assumption of its ubiquity and uniformity – the notion that an undifferentiated, ill-defined 'digital' is now the dominant form of contemporary mediation, and the primary mode of cultural production.[18] Another dominant idea is that the digital is fundamentally reducible to a conceptual logic of code, which allows it to exist as an immaterial concept that is separate from the material networks of hardware and screens that so often instantiate it.[19] This notion of the digital means that for many, the digital becomes visible, and therefore somehow material, only when it stops working, like many other kinds of infrastructure.[20] A third discourse that surrounds the digital is that of inauthenticity: the presumption that digital objects are defined by their capacities to be endlessly replicated, losing sight of any discourse of originality.[21] Finally, there is also a powerful discourse regarding the assumption that digital technologies are fundamentally social – that they are created not only to produce networks, but also are themselves networked, facilitating the production of networked public spheres, forms of communication and modes of collaboration and participation.[22] The social network is not simply a metaphor. Digital networks and social networks are often conflated or at least understood to be in a direct, mutually constitutive relationship. For example, in Chris Kelty's discussion of free and open source software projects, he argues that the open source project brings new publics, new codes and new legal systems into being simultaneously and as one and the same thing, which he describes as a 'recursive public'.[23] The social theory of digital networks argues that digital networks are not mere representations of social networks, but that they create, constitute, facilitate and perpetuate them.

These nascent theories of the digital, often emerging solely in dialogue with digital culture, share many key frameworks with material culture theory, much of which has emerged in museums. Both digital media and material culture theory posit that the 'object' of study – open source software, art, a pair of denim jeans – make people as much as they are made by people.[24] One of the fundamental arguments I am making here is that museum dialogues between digital technologies and museum collections allow us to both historicise and complicate many of our assumptions about digital technologies. We need to explore how digital objects are used to constitute reality effects, creating object lessons by altering and participating in how we both see and understand the world. This perspective allows us to unpack these assumptions of immateriality, abstraction, inauthenticity and sociality, leaving space to understand the politics of circulation, the material infrastructures and experiences of the digital, the challenges of obsolescence, and the inequality of access to digital worlds, among many other issues. Similarly, the work done to expose the authoritative epistemologies that are enshrined in museum technologies of collection, archiving and exhibition can help us unpack the ways in which social networks, collaboration and participation are curated by technical experts within digital platforms.

To bring this home, we might return to the American Museum of Natural History's Hall of Northwest Coast Indians. The oldest of the anthropological halls in the museum, it was originally conceived by Franz Boas in 1887, who drew on his experiences at the Chicago World's Fair and the Smithsonian Institution, as well his extensive field research on the Northwest Coast and collecting as part of the Jesup Expedition. Many visitors today assume the hall to have been preserved, almost unchanged, since then and, like the Pitt Rivers Museum, it has become an archetypal representation of a particular kind of early museum anthropology.[25] In fact, the display is now far removed from Boas' original conception of the hall as a palimpsest of different informational systems and forms of knowledge, in which singular objects, life groups, labels, photographs and expedition reports were presented in a multilayered way. Boas' vision was re-curated and significantly altered after he left the museum in 1905 by his successor Clark Wissler, who stripped out many of the objects to create a less cluttered style of display. Over the years, the famous canoe was moved from the ceiling to the floor outside the hall and was populated with life models, moving only recently back to the ceiling. Between 1910 and 1927, a series of romanticised murals depicting American Indian life painted by William S. Taylor were added to the walls. The Hall as we see it today seems to have changed little, its outdated spelling of tribal names and its dusty cases provoking both nostalgia from New Yorkers and frustration from many native peoples, but in fact it signals numerous interpretive and technological shifts over time. Over the years, the museum consistently prioritised other halls for refurbishment, rendering these halls and collections an outlier in a museum dedicated to geology, zoology, biodiversity and so on (missing an opportunity to narrate the human experience of the natural world). Yet the Hall has also been the site of an intensification of collaboration. Over time, the museum's anthropology department has developed its relationships with communities on the Northwest Coast, working to co-produce exhibitions, and on many other educational initiatives that are not visible within the exhibition halls.[26] Recently the museum launched an initiative, *Digital Totem*, an interactive screen aiming to 'bring contemporary Northwest

Coast voices and new interpretation into this historic gallery'.[27] Through the Web interface present in the gallery, visitors can meet native people through photographs and interviews, zoom into thirty objects from the collection, listen to local languages and create their own soundscapes drawing on sound recordings from the Northwest Coast.

The *Digital Totem* is part of a series of digital interventions in the hall, including the use of a *Video Bridge* robot that can bring native peoples from the Northwest Coast today into the hall and allow them to use the mobile robotic screen to move around while interacting with visitors.[28] Other projects include *Dreams of a Haida Child*, a collaboration with Haida artist Shoshannah Greene to develop a colouring book that uses augmented reality to link museum artefacts to Haida stories and landscapes.[29] These projects, at first glance, seem to fundamentally contrast with the unchanging character of the hall: the screens and apps render the collections that are scanned, augmented and socially framed more colourful, brighter, more tactile and more accessible than the same objects that lie still, either in their cases, hidden away with low lighting, or in the museum storerooms barely accessible to the public. These digital interventions seem to transform, improve, correct, enliven; yet they also depend on these collections for their existence, emerging from a deep engagement with the collections and their history, and from the recognition that the collections are vital and valuable cultural resources

Figure 12 Hall of Northwest Coast Indians with *Digital Totem*, 20 June 2017. Photograph by Matthew Shanley. ©AMNH/M.Shanley. Reproduced with permission.

Figure 13 Sean Young, collections curator at the Haida Gwaii Museum, engaging with visitors in the Hall of Northwest Coast Indians at the American Museum of Natural History using the *Video Bridge*, January 2016. Photograph reproduced with permission of Barry Joseph using a CC BY-NC-SA 2.0 licence.

for contemporary Northwest Coast peoples. Rather than assuming the digital to be a simple form of remediation and translation, we need to understand the complex processes of indexicality, mimesis and materiality that underscore these new museum practices, processes and cultural forms and understand the web of social relations that emerge between old and new forms of collections.

In October 2017, it was announced that the museum had finally decided to dedicate funds to comprehensively reconceptualise and reinstall the Hall. The efflorescence of digital projects, coupled with long-standing and sustained critique from native peoples was finally acknowledged by the museum as grounds for reinvestment. Peter Whiteley, curator of American Ethnology at the museum commented for the museum's press release: 'We eagerly look forward to working with First Nations communities to create a modern exhibition hall that we hope will serve as a new exemplar ... We want to build on a long history of dialogue with Native experts as we develop an updated installation with new understanding, transcending the boundaries that have too often divided museums and Native communities.'[30]

Cultural theories of digital objects

Our explorations of digital objects are often hampered by a series of assumptions about the digital that obscure its more 'ethnographic' realities. Part of the remit of the nascent field of digital anthropology is to denaturalise the digital, troubling the normative assumptions that tend not to be unpacked in other fields of enquiry. For instance, when we are told by Lev Manovich that software is 'a layer that permeates all areas of contemporary societies' and that it is increasingly constitutive of all cultural production, digital anthropologists might ask how this relationship could vary from place to place and be built up in very particular kinds of context.[31]

Jannis Kallinikos *et al.* argue that 'digital artefacts are intentionally incomplete and perpetually in the making' and that they have an ambivalent ontology.[32] I do not attempt here to rigidly define either digital media or digital objects, but rather aim to construct a more methodological argument around how to look at and understand the digital in context. This methodological blueprint should last far beyond the time specificity of any of the projects I will discuss in the book and can transcend the built-in obsolescence that defines many of the digital products and practices with which we are currently familiar. Kallinikos and his co-authors have set out in two papers a blueprint definition of digital artefacts. They argue that digital artefacts are characterised by being editable, interactive, open, reprogrammable and distributed, and that they are fundamentally granular and modular.[33] In an earlier article, I suggested that digital objects should be understood as situated within a continuum of mediation defined by an ongoing process of translation and remediation and a fundamental capacity for lateral connection.[34] We need to empirically explore these emerging forms and practices in order to recognise how many of Kallinikos' criteria are cultural values rather than intrinsic properties of the media or technology itself.

A growing body of digital anthropology is attentive to the situated ways in which technologies are located and co-produced by alternative preoccupations, sensibilities and cosmologies. Jennifer Deger's work within a media collective situated in the Northern Territory of Australia explores the ways in which Yolngu media practices instantiate Indigenous aesthetics, understandings of affect and world-making. The production and circulation of cellphone images, the repeated playing of Mariah Carey's 'All I Want for Christmas Is You' and the decoration of family graves and homes with store-bought stockings and tinsel at Christmas all enact Aboriginal forms of memorialisation, memory and ancestral form, co-opting these outside forms into an insider cosmological, discursive and aesthetic frame.[35]

Looking ethnographically at how people use and engage with digital objects makes it clear that these perceptions are not inherent to the nature or form of digital technologies alone, but also emerge from the ways in which these forms are appropriated and given meaning within very specific cultural locales. Ethnographic work can destabilise the certainties around the meaning of things, decentring the museum in favour of localised sites of interpretation. Compare two ethnographic accounts of the return to Pacific Island communities of 3D digital images from museum collections. In Graeme Were's account of the return of 3D Malanggan carvings to New Ireland (Papua New Guinea), the recognition that digital objects could not be touched or sensed in the same way as other collections facilitated a form of distancing that allowed Nalik people to internalise the images in order to reproduce them again locally and facilitate 'the reclamation, recovery and reintegration of cultural knowledge'.[36] Malanggan carvings are supposed to disappear after use, within what Susanne Küchler calls a 'sacrificial economy', which is why so many of them are now in museum collections.[37] Digital versions of Malanggan enable their reactivation within carving traditions, but they are not recognised as real enough to produce spiritual dissonance or to reawaken local knowledge claims.

By way of contrast, Deirdre Brown's account of several different projects to bring Māori *taonga* (which can be loosely translated as cultural treasures) into the digital domain demonstrates a dominant Māori discourse that insists on a seamless continuity between digital objects and their predecessors. Images of Māori ancestors, whether they be materialised in wood, stone, paper, on screens, in songs or in landscapes, are all valuable, existing within a shared cultural continuum.

In both New Zealand and New Ireland, digital collections are used to activate social relations and the transmission of cultural knowledge.[38] But the object worlds with which these digital platforms are understood to reside are very different. In a New Ireland context, the material form is less important than the knowledge that it inscribes. In a Māori context, each material context is considered as equal to any other, as Ngata *et al.* comment:

> *For people in Hauiti, however, the taonga-ness of an object, digital or otherwise, is determined by the quality of its relationships, so that something that to one person might appear as 'just an artefact'*

could be a taonga [cultural treasure] to someone who knows and/or is part of its history and kinship networks… Any artefact is a potential taonga, in the sense that it can be woven into the fabric of Hauiti whakapapa and knowledge, and any artefact creatively generated out of these relationships can be a taonga, no matter what its form. This includes digital objects: a hologram of the ancestral house Te Kani a Takirau is as much a taonga to people who know and/or are related to this ancestor and his or her history as the carved wooden panels from which it was made, that are now scattered among museums in New Zealand, the US and Europe. Reassembling these taonga digitally is therefore just as important – if not more so – as bringing them physically together.[39]

The return of a 3D digital version of a Malanggan in the British Museum therefore means something quite different in New Ireland to the return of a 3D Māori club from the Canterbury Museum in Christchurch. Nalik in New Ireland carefully kept the local property regimes that surround Malanggan away from digital images. Māori in the Northeast Coast of the North Island of New Zealand inscribe digital files with the same propriety and property relations as any other object. In both of these examples, digital media may be understood to oscillate between cultural worlds, bringing together multiple ways of knowing and being. Both of these examples provide different lessons in the cross-cultural interpretation of digital objects.

My perspective on interpreting the digital itself has emerged ethnographically, and has developed out of an involvement with many digital projects.[40] Questions of radical difference are at the heart of anthropology, and underpin the experience of numerous Indigenous peoples especially those living in settler-colonies.[41] Many of the most provocative interventions into the normativity of digital media and its effects started as political projects to 'decolonize the database' by co-opting digital media into projects not just of self-determination but of Indigenous world-making, where the Indigenous emerges as a foil for the production and recognition of radical difference.[42] For instance, it is no coincidence that many of the most creative refigurings of digital collection management systems have emerged in Australia, New Zealand and Canada, specifically to unsettle the archival imperatives, collecting paradigms, representational inequities and intellectual property claims of settler-colonial states. The Reciprocal Research Network (RRN), based at the Museum of Anthropology of the University of British Columbia, has created a consolidated collections database, drawing together collections from the Northwest Coast held in numerous museums around the world into one 'site' constructed primarily for Northwest Coast communities (and to a lesser extent, researchers) rather than an undifferentiated universal public.[43] Knowledge about artefacts can be shared and discussed, and then uploaded back into the original museum catalogues, potentially reconfiguring what is known, providing context, and in some cases new protocols for the care and management of objects.

In another example, Mukurtu is an open access collections management system that was developed by American anthropologist Kim Christen (now Kim Christen Withey) and colleagues out of her work with Warumungu Aboriginal communities in Tennant Creek, Australia. Starting as a digital project to think through the protocols around knowledge access in that specific community, Mukurtu now presents itself as 'a grassroots project aiming to empower communities to manage, share, and exchange their digital heritage in culturally relevant and ethically-minded ways'.[44] Local Contexts is an offshoot of Mukurtu led by Christen and Jane Anderson.[45] A hack of Creative Commons (itself a hack of copyright), Local Contexts produces licences and labels that facilitate both public awareness about, and allow for, the management of community protocols in relation to access and circulation of cultural expressions and knowledge. Labels such as TK Women Restricted, TK Attribution, TK Secret/Sacred and TK Commercial allow communities to appropriate representational, political and economic authority around the circulation of digital and digitised culture.[46]

These projects each demonstrate the ways in which digital tools allow communities to re-imagine museum protocols of knowledge management and circulation, redefining the social relations of entitlement and obligation that constitute archival property and propriety. They implicitly recognise the complicity of digital technologies within broader projects of colonial appropriation, in which archives have become vehicles of dispossession, and a space in which to negotiate sovereignty. As projects of resistance, then, these projects knowingly connect to broader discourses that frame the digital as open to remix and remastering, and link these to questions of accessibility and accountability. On the surface, these projects align with digital movements such as WikiLeaks and digital practices such as remix in that they appropriate digital capacities for circulation to challenge a singular point of curatorial authority.[47] The forms of cultural inflection I have been discussing also complicate the flattened 'public' constituted through projects such as Creative Commons. These projects raise an issue that Faye Ginsburg has described as a 'Faustian contract', as new media may bind Indigenous people to particular traditional identities, a bind Nancy Marie Mithlo has described as a 'red man's burden' (placing the burden of responsibility onto native peoples within museum collaborations).[48] Mithlo and Ginsburg have sensitively evaluated the role that Indigenous peoples play in institutional settings, recognising that new media does not necessarily entail new social and political relations and can in fact perpetuate old forms of inequality as well as producing new ones.

What compromises are necessitated through participation within these powerful zones of material engagement? How much are communities able to reconfigure not just the form but the structure of these complex assemblages that define both digital media and museums? Digital resources are currently creating new and complex materialities and permitting new kinds of access to collections. The opportunity to 3D print from high-resolution digital files has been picked up as a form of cultural return, for instance, in the case of the Tlingit, who have collaborated with the Smithsonian to print several objects from the collection of the National Museum of Natural History, allowing them to be recirculated and used back in communities.[49] In this context, 3D printing allows for objects to return simultaneously to several different communities. In other contexts, different forms of engagement are emerging surrounding the authenticity of these collections, contesting the status of digital files as museum or community property.[50]

A comparative, ethnographic approach, taken alongside the sensibility of material culture studies and museum anthropology, is very helpful in discussions of the otherwise amorphous and vast world of interest in digital media. This is but a single route into understanding the interpretive dilemmas and aesthetic sensibilities provoked by digital technologies, techniques and forms in museums. However, it is productive in that it allows us to challenge assumptions about the digital from the perspective of situated experience, and to understand this experience as produced by systems and structures that exist outside of the digital. By thinking of digitisation as a cultural process of interpretation and meaning-making, we can open up what has often been radically naturalised in both museum and digital environments. It is this naturalisation that creates what I call throughout the volume 'reality effects' – the perceptions of the real that are actually carefully constructed and produced through a wide range of media. In museums, reality effects are vital to the production of object lessons. The rest of this volume is dedicated to an exploration of these issues as they ripple across the surface of, and reverberate within, a series of objects that themselves refract across different media, and take multiple forms.

3
Box

Figure 14 An empty lantern-slide box from the UCL Ethnography Collection used in the *Sawdust and Threads* project 2015. © Caroline Wright. Reproduced with permission.

In order to fully unpack how object lessons work in museums and within digital media, we need to understand fully how knowledge is built up from objects, what interpretive frames we use, and the ways in which they bring particular views of the object into being. We need to be scholars of material culture, understanding the social significance of objects and the ways in which the organisation of things mirrors the epistemologies and classificatory principles that enable us to understand the world. We also need to understand collections as materials – as forms and substances that generate sensuous and embodied knowledge. It is for this reason that I chose to start my explorations of contemporary object lessons in front of a simple wooden box. The box was manufactured by Johnsons of Hendon; it was made of carefully jointed pine, held together with brass hinges and was kept closed using small brass hooks. The box is papered inside with lined and numbered cards, allowing an interior cataloguing of a numbered collection of lantern-slides held within the pine grooves. From the picture, you can see the box may seem empty, but as I will discuss, it is in fact remarkably full. This wooden box is a contact zone, a material mediator between collections and ideas, people and things, modes of analysis and forms of experience. It is a container of knowledge and a provoker of questions.

I had never looked at the box until the project *Sawdust and Threads*, initiated by the artist Caroline Wright. Working with the Scott Polar Institute of Cambridge University, and across the museums and collections of University College London, Wright asked to be given deaccessioned artefacts from each of these collections. She proceeded to make delicate pencil drawings of each of the objects on uniformly sized paper, and then, sitting in public spaces within the university and museums and using only hand tools, she took apart the original artefacts, until all that was left was 'sawdust and threads'. Wright's project was an explicit excavation of value and meaning, asking if they are located within the form of objects or in the systems of classification and museum protocols that surround them. By tracking between objects, drawings and back to (decomposed) objects, the project also explored the materiality of objects over time and across different media. In the following sections I explore how collections-based research builds up very particular forms of knowledge around objects, drawing out our assumptions about the relations between meaning and matter, form and content. These object lessons, I argue, are vital for understanding the resonance of digital objects.

How do we know things?

> *It is time to see a materially focused, material culture studies back in the centre of museum practice and museum studies. It has not held such a place since the late nineteenth century and it deserves to return – not in the positivist, static form and role it held in the past, but through a gentle twenty-first-century revolution in which the object is once more at the heart of the museum, this time as a material focus of experience and opportunity, a subtle and nuanced, constructed, shifting thing, but also physical, ever-present, beating pulse of potential, quickening the museum and all that it is and could be.*[1]

The object lesson, as it emerged in the nineteenth-century ethnographic collection, drew together material form and theory into seemingly cohesive narrative form. Twentieth-century museologies have focused on unravelling these narratives, exposing the power relations, collecting practices and, often, the colonial injustices that underpinned them. Objects have been reconnected to communities who have been given opportunities to present, and represent, their own ideas and narratives. However, over the course of the twentieth century, following the dominant ways of thinking about interpretation and representation, anthropology and other disciplines separated words and objects.[2] Museums by definition have resisted this divorce, notwithstanding Brown Goode's invocation to make all displays a collection of well-written labels illustrated by objects (see p. 11 of this volume). As multisensory environments, where words jostle with things, museums make an implicit argument that knowledge emerges out of objects, experience and interpretation. In the twenty-first century, this interpretive complexity has returned to our understanding of how knowledge is created in the world, and museums and collections have been re-centred as sites of investigation within a new interdisciplinary framework, that draws together this renewed attention to the interpretive entanglements of form and meaning.[3]

The end of the twentieth century generated a number of new museologies. The first signalled a re-exploration of museum publics and visitors, opening up the collections and exhibitions to new communities of interest and new stakeholders. There was also a shift of understanding of the museum visitor, from the nineteenth-century model of the public citizen to a twentieth-century rendition of the citizen as consumer. Digital media has been deeply implicated within this museology, used as a tool of participation to better integrate the museum visitor within a consumer experience and within new social frameworks. The resurgence of interest in materiality, and emphasis on consumerism, has also precipitated another museology – one that pays renewed attention to valued objects as well as their constituencies. The publication of popular books such as Neil MacGregor's *A History of the World in 100 Objects*, the growing popularity of craft and maker-movements and the continued debates over repatriation insist on an epistemological focus on objects as well as people but also show us how salient consumer culture is to this perspective.[4]

Material museologies

This dual orientation towards objects has engendered a renewed interest in materials as sites of both production and consumption. In 2012, the

Figure 15 Selection of world clays dug by volunteers with the Clayground Collective at a clay and ceramics open day at the Institute of Making, 24 October 2015. Reproduced with permission of the Institute of Making under a CC-BY license.

UCL Faculty of Engineering opened the Institute of Making, a workshop and idiosyncratic materials library, available for use by anyone at the university. The Institute of Making is part laboratory, part make-space, part artist project and part archive. The materials library draws together a collection of materials both new and old, and hosts 'materials of the month' in which large quantities of materials, such as coal, are made available for experimentation. Its shelves hold bells cast in different metals, lumps of latex plus small glass vials containing such delights as radioactive material, as well as the baby teeth of one of the founders, Zoe Laughlin. The objects are displayed on open shelving so that they can be touched and picked up, and many can be used experimentally: chipped, smashed, heated, frozen. The materials library is the gateway to a make-space, and as such it aims to encourage the exploration of materials through making, to embed materials and making into a wide variety of research contexts, to encourage making as a constituent component of academic practice. Where the Pitt Rivers Museum's typological strategy was curated in order to theorise evolutionary hierarchy within the relationship between technology and society, the Institute of Making is an argument for embedding materials knowledge and workshop skills within academic research and enquiry and promotes the frame of material science – of understanding the nature of materials – as an experimental and creative approach towards the production of new kinds of object.[5]

This material museology argues in many ways against many of the traditional values of museums: collections are seen as dynamic, unfolding and subject to repeated interpretation. Their meanings are constantly evolving. Knowledge is not fixed within narrative, nor does it need to be located in cultural or historical context. In the Institute of Making, materials precede artefacts. They generate knowledge through what Tim Ingold has described as 'sensory perception and practical engagement', rather than through the engagement of a detached 'mind with the material world', which presumes an overly determined divide between a disembodied mind and an external reality.[6]

What are the consequences to this analytic move from material culture studies (and the relationship between people and material that it suggests) towards a focus on materials (in which culture is suddenly rendered outside of materials)? Is it possible to translate this vanguard of anthropological theorisation into a way of understanding collections, and can it help us to understand the place of digital objects in museums? This shift away from the 'context' to the 'form' of the object mirrors current trends in scholarship that focus on 'materials' and 'materiality' rather than 'material culture', and by extension on doing and making as well as looking. This perspective is strongly argued for by Tim Ingold, who has critiqued the notion of 'material culture' in favour of an emphasis on 'materials', which he defines as being better focused on 'the stuff that things are made of'.[7] Ingold's position has engendered a series of lively debates around the methodology and practice of interpreting objects.[8] Ingold wishes to move away from an understanding of materials as entirely encircled by human culture, advocating for an a priori perspective on materials, which then become entangled with people, generating material experiences and the transformative processes of making.

The decomposition of material cultures into materials acts as a kind of distillation, purifying the historical trajectories of individual artefacts into generic materials, which exist a priori as somehow 'raw' material that we may then transform into worthy things. For instance, a well-received book by Mark Miodownik, Professor of Material Science and one of the founders of the Institute of Making, entitled *Stuff Matters*, starts with the single image of the author drinking afternoon coffee on the roof of his apartment building in London.[9] Miodownik breaks down this tableau into its material components, dedicating chapters of his book to concrete, glass, chocolate and porcelain. In each chapter, he explores the development of these materials into the artefacts on his rooftop tableau and he traces the emergence of these materials into human projects. Within this narrative, humans are presented as romantically enthralled by the possibilities of material science. Miodownik celebrates the transformational capacity of human ingenuity to work with raw materials. This kind of focus on materials ignores a grand tradition in anthropology, from Sidney Mintz's paradigmatic exploration of sugar, through to Anna Tsing's work on Matsutake mushrooms in which materials are understood to be deeply embedded within human lifeworlds – not simply part of raw nature, but themselves embedded as much in culture, implicated in broader political or global systems in which human subjectivity and matter continually make and remake each other.[10]

In a recent volume, *The Social Life of Materials*, Adam Drazin and Susanne Küchler argue for a perspective on materials that sees materials not as 'the raw stuff from which people would be able to shape cultural and social life' but as social, embedded within culture as much as within nature.[11] Mintz's classic account of our taste for sugar, *Sweetness and Power*, emphasises the mutuality of relationships between peoples and things, arguing that the excessive consumption of sugar is both the symptom and the cause of plantation capitalism and that our taste for sweetness is as much cultural and political as it is biological. Tsing's account of Matsutake mushrooms explores a highly valued fungal form that is a consequence of plantation capitalism and the impact of human consumption on forest ecologies that have in turn created new political economies and conditions for nature.

Teaching through things

The oscillation of analytic focus from the meanings embedded within material forms (or platforms), or those that emerge from their participation in wider social worlds, long predates the digital age. If the received history of museum object lessons focuses on the public entanglement of collections and exhibitions, teaching collections provide us with a very different perspective on object lessons, one in which there is less preoccupation with formal narratives of exhibition, and a greater emphasis on knowing through making, doing and use. A teaching collection imparts a very different kind of object lesson to those experienced from the vantage point of the exhibition hall. Instead of presenting a curated narrative of objects to educate the visitor, the teaching collection is a material entanglement of complex discussions and affords more intimate engagements with objects as they may be handled, taken apart, put together, played, worn or used as they were first intended to be used. In the UCL Ethnography Collections, such intimacies, combined with a lack of context, provenance or external information about the collection have pushed us to explore what we can learn through the surface encounter with the form of the object itself, rather than the usual contexts within which we situate objects (cultural, archival or collection contexts). Teaching collections can allow us to denaturalise many of the narratives that form part of exhibitions and that structure our more spectacular engagements with collections.

The Ethnography Collections were created by the first chair of anthropology at UCL, Darryl Forde, and were from the start intended primarily for teaching. The collections, comprising nearly 2,500 objects from all parts of the world, were drawn together from a number of disparate sources. In a 2008 collections survey it was discovered that only 32 per cent of the collections have any clear provenance.[12] Since it was founded in the 1940s, the Ethnography Collections have continued to grow through donations and gifts from missionary and learned societies, alumnae, and anthropologists and students working in the department. Its curators are academics and it is very much a working collection, a part of every student experience from their first year in the department. Until very recently there was no formal exhibition space: the collection was stored within a seminar room where students and staff could interact with objects far away from the eyes of professional curators or conservators. Now, following contemporary trends in material culture studies, we are more likely to be teaching courses focusing on the poetics of different materials, or welcoming source communities to the collection than we are to be using the objects to learn about 'primitive modes of production', one of the signature courses established by Forde.

The Ethnography Collections' character is perhaps best encapsulated by one distinct group of objects, which in fact were all deaccessioned from another collection. This group comprises nearly 300 objects from around the world that were given to UCL between 1951 and 1964. These were part of the 'ethnographic collection' of the Wellcome Institute, objects that were understood to be disconnected from the Institute's mission of collecting medical culture and history in a global context but that formed part of Henry Wellcome's ambition to create a 'Museum of Man'.[13] Many of these objects were dispersed after Henry Wellcome's death, in 1936, to a wide range of universities and museums in a series of gifts.[14] Somehow, upon their dispersal, many of the objects were separated from their catalogue details, so all we know about them comes from the circular handwritten labels carefully fastened to each one. These labels indicate that one object is a 'Māori cloak', another a 'Kuba knife'.

When objects entered the collection, Forde classified them according to his teaching taxonomies, so the cloak became part of a selection of

Figure 16 A Māori flint adze, once part of the Wellcome Collection. E.0062. UCL Ethnography Collections. Photograph by Haidy Geismar. © UCL Reproduced under a CC-BY licence.

'textiles', and the knife part of 'knives, swords, spears, spearthrowers'. As object lessons, the Ethnography Collections were largely unmoored from their location within both fieldwork methodologies and collection histories. Rather, they were drawn together as three-dimensional illustrations for lectures and classes, and were also used to instantiate an underlying theory about objects and embodied forms of knowledge through the process of production or making. The motley assortment of objects from the Wellcome Collection was certainly one strand underpinning the emergence of material culture studies at UCL. The collection was used by scholars such as Forde, Mary Douglas and Michael Rowlands to teach courses focused on the technologies of specific regions, and was often used to instantiate a Marxist perspective on production as a lens to understanding culture and society. The artefacts were used as exemplars of agriculture, locomotion, ironmaking and weaving. They were understood to exemplify 'modes of production' that were seen as constitutive of diverse forms of social organisation and of aesthetic traditions. Objects in this context were understood as meaningful because of what they were made to do within societies around the world, illustrating the functionalist approach that underpinned this nascent Marxist museology.

In 2012 we convened a group of staff and students at UCL to explore the different ways of understanding and interpreting objects in a research group called *Properties and Social Imagination*.[15] Working with the Ethnography Collections, we chose three artefacts, selected specifically because they were perceived to fall into three discrete categories of material: stone, cloth and wood. We divided into three groups, each focused on one of the artefacts: a prehistoric greenstone adze from Papua New Guinea, a piece of nineteenth-century barkcloth from Sulawesi and a wooden spearthrower made in the nineteenth century by Aboriginal Australians. Our brief was to explore the nature of research, starting with the object, challenging the idea that meaning and context could be projected from other sources. We asked what could be known from the form itself, testing Ingold's hypothesis about materials. Each group explored how they might generate culturally specific knowledge, from the starting and vantage point of the object itself, imagined for the project as defined by an outwardly apprehended material form.[16]

I was part of the team working with the barkcloth. We explored the nature of barkcloth as a laid rather than woven fabric, comparing it to both Tyvek and to the paper dresses of 1960s Carnaby Street. We found out about a conservation project at UCL that examined paper objects by monitoring their smell, deducing their stability through their interaction with their environments by analysing the molecules that they emit. We took the barkcloth to the research laboratory in the UCL Institute for Sustainable Heritage and left it in one of their bell jars for several days. We found that even at a molecular level it had no smell.[17] The chemical printout from the project confirmed a property of the material: that it was remarkably absorbent and inert. This property resonated quietly with the ways in which barkcloth has been traditionally put to use in places such as Indonesia and the Pacific Islands, where its qualities of absorbency (through its lack of smell) and strength (through the laid nature of the textile) produce a material that, as a wrapper for the body, mediates the living and the dead, and is drawn into exegetical discourses that describe barkcloth as a kind of second skin.[18]

This conceptual, pedagogical and methodological shift back and forth from material culture to materials critiques the tendency of previous interpretive projects to incessantly convert objects into symbols,

Figure 17 Barkcloth being measured for emissions at the UCL Institute of Sustainable Heritage. Photograph by Haidy Geismar.

understood through representational projects, and described through language, and more recently code. By taking objects seriously 'in their own terms', a materials-oriented perspective implicitly critiques the hermeneutics of museum processes of working with collections, which starts with singular artefacts collected in particular historical and social moments, absorbs them into wider collections and in so doing constitutes 'generic' knowledge about culture and society that transcends the moments of their collection and, in turn, draws further objects, no matter their provenance, into this context. A specific cloak comes to stand for all cloaks, and therefore defines the next cloak that is collected.

However, a focus on materials has the potential to evacuate the specificities of the interpretive moment of encounter and naturalise all kinds of cultural assumptions, privileging an unchallenged analytic authority rather than a culturally and located process of interpretation. Within the Properties project we quickly discovered that our original definitions of materials as properties had all sorts of assumptions built into them. We learned that our division of objects into three 'natural kinds' – stone, cloth and wood – was misleading and unhelpful when we came to think about what we as anthropologists rather than as materials scientists could bring to a greater understanding of these artefacts. In fact, our focus on materials undid our own categories. We discovered that barkcloth was strong like stone, that stone was soft like wood, and that wood was shiny like stone. We discovered this not simply through a sensuous engagement with the materials, but through a renewed attention to material culture in which we explored the uses to which these materials had been put and their resonance in different social and cultural settings. It is no coincidence then that the industrial laid textile Tyvek is used not only in industrial contexts, where it is valued for its strength, but that it has also become the material used for surgical scrubs and paper underwear. Its unique strength and absorbency make it ideal to be laid next to the human body, just as barkcloth is used as mortuary wrapping in the Pacific Islands. It was challenging for the students and staff alike to rethink our understanding of the relationship between objects and their contexts and to understand how useful knowledge could emerge from artefacts alone without locating them in multiple contexts of scholarly literature, collection histories and local environments of production, use and care. The attention to materials was productive only in as much as it led us to unpick the assumptions that were built into our classificatory systems and ways of understanding the collections, relocating them in a more expansive social and material context.

Box

Sawdust and Threads posed a conceptual challenge from the start, challenging the history of defining and valuing objects in the collection by focusing on the value of objects that had been deaccessioned. As far as I am aware, the Ethnography Collections have never formally deaccessioned an object, and being a collection without a museum, we have no formal criteria for how this could be done. Indeed, as the Wellcome Collection dispersal demonstrates, the Ethnography Collection is a place that has welcomed deaccessioned objects from other places. Shifts in our collections management towards a greater interest in conservation, alongside the contemporary interests of material culture studies, mean that every dropped fibre or flake gets put in its own bag or box, and becomes part of the collection. As objects slowly disintegrate over time, so the collection expands infinitely, limited only by space.

Our conundrum, then – that we have no experience of deaccessioning and that every object has some research potential in our collection – initially seemed to mean that we would not be able participate in Wright's project. But, as I looked around the collection, I started to think more carefully about the ways in which collections and institutions define the boundaries of what is even recognisable as part of a collection. The object I selected for Wright to work with, a simple wooden box, demonstrates not just the fragility of objects and their value, but also the fragility of the classificatory schemes and taxonomies that underpin them.

Figure 18 Fragments of UCL Ethnography Collection. Part of a project by Jasmine Popper, MA student in Material and Visual Culture at UCL. Reproduced with permission.[19]

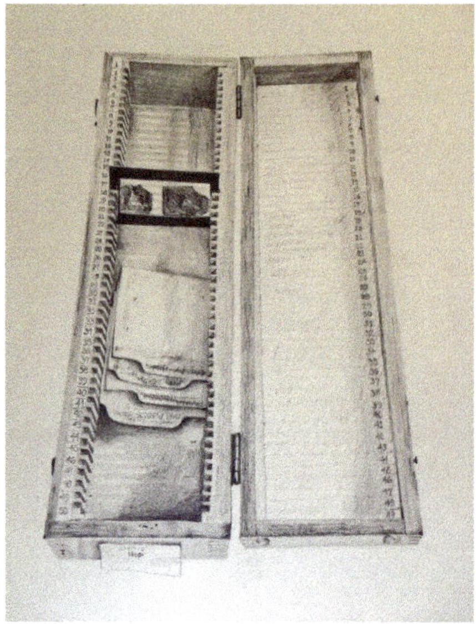

Figure 19, 20, 21 Transforming the lantern-slide box. Caroline Wright, *Sawdust and Threads*, 2015. Mixed media, pencil on paper. © Caroline Wright. Reproduced with permission.

The wooden box, constructed to hold glass lantern-slides, is one of several identical boxes currently sitting on a high shelf in the collection. Lantern-slide lectures can be seen as early PowerPoint presentations. They gathered together photographs from the field, photographs of objects and photographs of photographs, as well as photographs of pages from books. They did the work of image libraries, intensifying the relationship between material, visual and discursive knowledge. In the form of the lantern-slide, all of these images become uniform on the visual plane of the square glass plate. Lantern-slides were used in lecturing and teaching well into the 1950s, when they were gradually supplanted by smaller transparencies, acetate film and, eventually, digital projectors. At UCL we have copies of lectures that provide the caption list for some of the lantern-slides that show us how our forebears made sense of the objects in the collection by providing contexts – the slides show objects in use, in place, in relation to similar artefacts, and situate them within broader cultural worlds through magical projections.[20]

The wooden slide boxes now sit empty on high shelves in the collection. The slides themselves have shifted in our value system from being reproduced and reproducible images to being unique and singular historical artefacts. Because of this they have been catalogued and now rest in individual acid-free mounts and boxes, next to their original homes. Our box itself is currently caught in an out-of-time moment. In ten years, when we have perhaps moved to bigger premises and have more space, it might also become an 'object' valued for the historical resonances it holds as an artefact of material culture theory and teaching. At this time, I suggest that it has been conceptually deaccessioned. It has been studied carefully by our student volunteers, and all of the information deemed relevant or important – the handwriting on the inside of the lid that indicated what slides went where and in what order – has been digitally transcribed and added to the digital catalogue. The materiality of the box – its colour, its feel, its texture, its own geometry – is currently of little interest (although interest has, paradoxically, grown out of Wright's project). Its materiality has been negated (just as the materiality of the slides within has been recognised anew). I say this provocatively, because it was with some difficulty that I took the decision to give the object to Caroline's project (with appropriate consultation within the department and with UCL Museums and Collections). I am slightly appeased by the knowledge that we have other, similar boxes, still sitting on the shelves. But my commitments to the material form of objects still whisper in my ear, asking: 'But what of this specific box? Its singularity, its own form?' and my own experiences as a museum researcher have taught me that we may yet have much to uncover about this box. We have yet to discover whose handwriting recorded the order of the slides (it was only after the project that someone whispered in my ear that it was probably Darryl Forde's) and in what academic debates this material manifestation of an academic lecture participated. We have yet to discover interests we cannot at this time imagine.

The box, even emptied of its contents, thus sits out of time but pregnant with poignancy and potential. It is both an object and a source of information, although its status as an object is currently precarious. In the present moment, information can migrate into digital catalogues and descriptions, and this supplanted materiality can be discarded. Indeed, Caroline herself has taken apart the box, grinding it down to a pile of red dust and a handful of rivets. Yet, in her drawing we have a lifeline to that materiality, and also an expression of the tension around recognition, classification and value that sits in the very form of objects themselves. What will be recognised from that drawing in the future? Can the drawing become the object? How is the drawing different from the digital notes now representing the box in the database? The hesitant ephemerality of pencil on paper seems to contrast to the original solidity of the wooden box, yet we had already dismantled that box before we gave it to Caroline. We had stripped away its meaning, separated meaning from form, dissolved writing into digital text, and stripped away both wonder and resonance from the box itself. Indeed, while it may not be attached to a complex bureaucratic process, we have thoroughly conceptually deaccessioned this particular box.

Wright's drawing coexisted with the box for almost a year. Both were displayed in the project's final exhibition at Norwich Castle Art Museum, alongside the other objects in various stages of decomposition.[21] Then, Wright returned to UCL, where she sat in the lobby of the anthropology department for several days at a makeshift workbench, and slowly worked the object out of its form. It took her a long time to muster the resolve. Students and staff walking to exams, lectures and supervisions might have caught a glimpse of the moments in which she smashed the glass slide with a small hammer, or were drawn into conversation with Wright as she sanded the well-made box down into a red dust.

The archaeologist Severin Fowles has suggested that within the so-called 'material turn', objects have been made subject to a kind of interpretive colonisation. He goes so far as to suggest that objects have emerged within anthropology as the new subalterns – a silent, disempowered constituency over which we, as analysts, assert academic supremacy, whether it be around the process of interpretation or the methodologies we use to undertake research.[22] The oscillation of focus between materials and material culture therefore speaks to a series of much broader issues of interpretation that are extremely important in museums and are also equally important in the ways in which we make sense of digital media.[23] Do we focus our attention on the form of the box or its contents? Where do we draw the line between the two? How do we define the differences between a reproduction and an original? Is this a material or social distinction? These questions challenge us to consider the politics of our analytic framework, the terms of engagement with both artefacts and the people and ideas that we believe them to represent, and the ways in which we locate context both in and out of the collection. The idea of *affordances* has been appropriated instrumentally into design practice, and a host of disciplined frameworks that focus on 'users' (e.g. human–computer interaction, interaction design, design thinking). The co-option of this concept as instrumental to the creation of new and better products should not blind us to the way in which James Gibson developed the notion of affordances within an ecological perspective, in which artefacts are understood to have specific potentials situated in material and social environments. For Gibson, an affordance is the interaction between an object, its user and its environment, all of which determines the possibility of its use. This is also fundamentally a contextual approach demanding an understanding of two scales (the social and material).[24]

At the end of the project, all that was left of the box was a framed drawing and a pile of dust and rivets. Wright plans to mix the dust into paint to create new images. The box now sits wrapped in paper in my office as we wait for our collection space to be improved. I will use this drawing as a warning: it will sit in the collection as a continued reminder that in every material form there is value, even if we cannot, at that moment, see it. As the first object lesson of this book, the box teaches us that debates about shifting value, visual perception and materiality long predate the digital. In the chapters that follow I track how the forms of a pen, an effigy and a cloak are refracted across different media, instantiating different cultural values and perspectives. Each of these, following the example of the box, is an object lesson into the limits of materials, and the continued oscillation of object and information, that produce knowledge in museum collections.

4
Pen

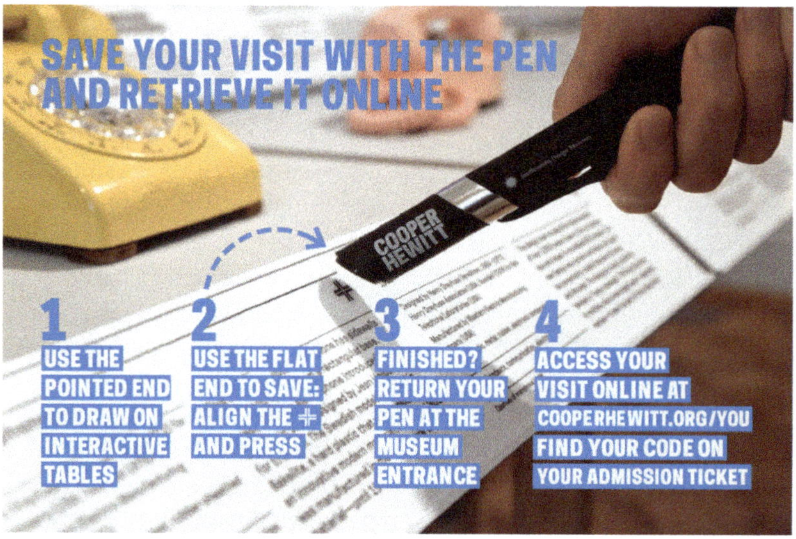

Figure 22 The Cooper Hewitt Pen promotional postcard.
Source: https://www.cooperhewitt.org/events/current-exhibitions/using-the-pen/. Reproduced from website under fair use.

> *It lets you collect everything. Use it on our tables to learn and play. Return the Pen before you leave but keep your ticket so you can see what you've collected. Any time, anywhere.*

The empty lantern-slide box, now decomposed into a pile of dust plus a drawing, is an object lesson in understanding the complex entanglement of matter and meaning, and the role that remediation and visualisation play in this process. The project's focus on handwork and craft (Wright's skilful drawing and the physical dissolution of the box) is helpful in signalling how I think we should be looking at the production of digital objects: as skilled, culturally located material practices of objectification.

My second object instantiates this perspective, highlighting how an entirely 'new' digital object – a device aimed at creating a new form of interactivity for the museum visitor drawing on the power of museum databases, web interfaces and digital imaging – embodies long-standing ways of looking at collections and thinking about design.

The Pen has become integral to the visitor experience at the Cooper Hewitt Museum of Design in New York, extending the object lessons of the decorative arts museum. When the Cooper Hewitt Museum, now a part of the Smithsonian Institution, reopened after a massive overhaul in spring 2015, the Pen was a focal point for the recalibration of the collections. This sleek black wand was presented as a saviour of the collection, making an artefact out of the visitor experience, bringing coherence to the design project that was started more than 100 years ago.

Designing design

Housed in the former mansion of Andrew Carnegie on Fifth Avenue, part of New York City's Museum Mile, the Cooper Hewitt Museum houses a collection gathered by the family of Peter Cooper, who established a Museum for the Arts of Decoration in downtown New York City at the Cooper Union

Figure 23 Cooper Union Museum's Metalwork Gallery, c. 1945. © Smithsonian Institution Archives. Image # SIA2011-2177. Reproduced with permission.

in 1895. Like the Victoria and Albert (V&A) Museum in London and the Musée des Arts Décoratifs in Paris, the Cooper Hewitt was established as a working collection for the modern designer – a storehouse of techniques and forms to be used as both inspiration and object lessons in understanding, style and modes of production of artists, craftspeople and designers. These collections define design as both a creative and an industrial exercise, bound up in the transformations of craft in the nineteenth century, and referencing the imperial and colonial appropriation of materials and traditions in order to develop new national styles.[1] Design and decorative arts in this museum world were presented as the careful balance between handwork, machine-work, authorship and practical knowledge, all in the service of bettering national trajectories of manufacture, and by extension of encouraging the taste of a new generation of consumers.

Museums of decorative arts (many are now also called museums of art and design) emerged in the nineteenth century at the nexus of industrial manufacture and presented a nationalist retelling of histories of artisanal skill in this emerging reconfiguration of craft. At the moments when many critics, led by the writings of John Ruskin and William Morris, perceived handcraft to be under threat from modern machines, the decorative arts museum reinvented craft for the machine age, balancing notions of the artisanal with the emerging field of industrial design.[2] Museums such as the Victoria and Albert in London were expressly designed to expand the scope of collecting in the dual contexts of industrialisation and imperialism, to be used actively in the training of new manufacturers and designers, and to build the taste of middle-class consumers.[3] Many understood the South Kensington Museum complex in London, and the Government Schools of Design attached to it, as a palimpsest of art and industry. Tim Barringer describes it as, 'redolent of the modernity of international exhibitions, the department store, liberal economics, technical design education and utilitarian reform ideology', alongside the more traditional functions of museums.[4]

When the Cooper Union, a free school for adults dedicated to both science and art, was founded it was Peter Cooper's intention that it include a museum. At that time (1859), the only other museums in New York were the New York Historical Society and P.T. Barnum's Museum downtown on the Bowery, both of which had a very different flavour and ethos.[5] Cooper wanted to establish a teaching museum that would enable, in practical terms, the perpetuation of the craft and decorative arts traditions.[6] The museum was finally opened by Cooper's granddaughters in 1897, and was co-located on the fourth floor of the Cooper Union with the Women's Art School. From its inception, the Cooper Hewitt Museum was conceived as a 'visual library' and a 'practical working laboratory' in which 'objects could be touched, moved, sketched, photographed, and measured'.[7] The Hewitt sisters travelled regularly to Europe and drew on their circle of friends and philanthropists such as J.P. Morgan to support their collecting activities. They not only collected objects, but also made 'encyclopaedic' scrapbooks in which they collated pictures of all forms of the decorative arts, with the intention that they be used as source books for design.[8]

The collection was framed as a 'laboratory' for the designer/craftsperson, and as such was arranged for ease of comparison across styles, periods and media. Visitors were encouraged to learn by drawing on pads and pencils that were scattered throughout the collection, and the museum was kept open in the evenings to allow for working people and students to visit. Objects were displayed chronologically and by styles of ornamentation, with the explicit intention that even if the labels were not read, a visual progression was obvious.[9] This sense of progression was intended to influence the work of designers who visited the collections, following the models of the museum's counterparts in London and Paris. Such display strategies also echoed the typological display and influence of ideas about social evolution that were being developed at around the same time in ethnographic museums such as the Pitt Rivers and the United States National Museum in Washington D.C., and at world's fairs and expositions, all of which were collectively influential in founding the ethnographic, scientific and art collections of the mid-nineteenth century.[10]

Over time, the museum amassed an enormous collection of prints, drawings, textiles, furnishings, furniture, jewellery and other decorative arts, becoming the largest such collection in the USA. By the 1960s the Cooper Union could no longer sustain the collection and it was transferred to the Smithsonian's care on the condition that it remain in New York City. By 1976 the collection of more than 210,000 objects was installed and opened to the public in the Andrew Carnegie Mansion on 91st street and Fifth Avenue.

Surface images: Object lessons of the decorative arts

The so-called arts of decoration, as they are imagined within museums such as the Cooper Hewitt, might be argued as pre-empting the digital era in the ways in which they create lateral connections across time and space by visually tracing surface patterns across objects. This emphasis on surface pattern, and the inscription of image into material, is one way in which the process of design has come to be defined. The Hewitt sisters were just as interested in books and prints as they were in textiles and bird cages. For instance, they went out of their way to collect volumes such as Audubon's *Birds of America*, to be used as a reference work for the bird motif across textiles, china, architectural mouldings and so on.[11] Over time, the collection has expanded to include photographs and slides and, later, digital images and software.

In this museological context, the notion of design was underwritten by ideas about prototype objects or plans for future objects; was defined as a practice of making; established a blueprint for makers; and a form of curation (a bringing together of styles, motifs and materials). The anthropology of design and decoration has defined design as a social technology, linking 'the material basis of things, their material qualities … or affordances, and their social context'.[12] In many ways, the notion of the decorative arts draws an object lesson out of the image library: understanding museum collections as a gathering of images that could migrate across media in the service of design. Seen in this way, the genre of decorative arts fuses a past-oriented fine-arts aesthetic with a commitment to industrial modernisation and consumer capitalism rippling through the surface of the image. The Cooper Hewitt and other decorative arts collections combined the civic intentions of museums with the enthusiasms of industrial innovation.[13]

Museum studies have focused on decorative arts museums as crucibles of changing cultural values around industrial production, linking romantic visions of past craft to modern-day commodities, and inculcating through hand and eye work the formation of taste in the museum visitor as well as influencing the process of industrial design. This theory assumes museum collections and display have the power, and the authority, to influence production.[14] In his account of the industrial art and design education program at the Metropolitan Museum of Art in New York in the 1920s, Trask argues against this theory of influence in describing the collection of decorative arts: 'whilst attempting to break new aesthetic ground, the museum was simply a resource library, rather than an industrial art or craft academy like the Deutscher Werkbund or Bauhaus Schools in Germany'.[15] Trask highlights how, rather than being blueprints for manufacture, the image of design presented in museums was one primarily for consumption by the middle classes, training them to appreciate designed objects and aspire to collect them at home. Objects were understood as images, their designs and colours appropriated from the surface of one object onto another (from a textile to a lamp, or a curtain to a carpet).

The Cooper Hewitt collection may be read as sitting somewhere in between these two types of museum, although it could also be argued that the move uptown pushed the collection's ethos more towards reifying

Figure 24 *Greek no. 7: Ornaments from Greek and Etruscan vases in the British Museum and the Louvre*. From *The Grammar of Ornament* by Owen Jones (1856). Illustrated by examples from various styles of ornament; 100 folio plates, drawn on stone by F. Bedford; and printed in colours by Day and son. The Miriam and Ira D. Wallach Division of Art, Prints and Photographs: Art & Architecture Collection, The New York Public Library. Retrieved from https://digitalcollections.nypl.org/items/510d47da-3a97-a3d9-e040-e00a18064a99, out of copyright.

design rather than supporting the work of craftspeople. The complex fusing of the object as image within the decorative arts collection was part of a broader museological move towards the image as object, underpinned by the emerging technologies of reproduction. Photography, electrotyping and casting all created new ways of collecting, circulating and knowing objects in museums.[16]

Alongside the object lessons that these projects can teach us about the migration of images across forms and their role in producing patterns of culture, the collection of copies, both in the form of images and objects, has long been perceived to be part of a project to democratise access to museum collections. In contrast to the trajectory of the fine arts, which over the course of the twentieth century used the foil of authenticity, originality and artistic genius to value collections, techniques of industrial manufacture gave rise to a new genre of museum collection explicitly realised as collections of copies. In a similar vein to the ways in which we talk about websites and online collections databases as opening access to museum collections, plaster casts and other reproductions were understood in the nineteenth and early twentieth centuries as means to provide access to world heritage that would otherwise be fixed in place. In 1867, the V&A's director, Henry Cole, drafted the 'International Convention of Promoting Universally Reproductions of Works of Art' and persuaded several European princes to sign up to a project that involved sharing reproductions of important works as they gathered at the Paris International Exhibition of that year.[17] The convention paved the way for the establishment of new ways of understanding the value of reproductions in museums. Plaster casts enabled access to the 'old world' in the 'new world', breaking down divides between the centre and the periphery. Not every regional museum could provide its visitors with access to the great canonical masterpieces of European art unless it was accepted that the plaster cast was not just a substitute but an indexical conduit to the real thing.[18] The architectural hall, or Cast Courts, of the V&A museum is one of the most celebrated examples of this drive to collect reproductions, with life-size casts of classical antiquities, some – such as the copy of Trajan's Column in Rome – so large that they had to be displayed in two parts and dictated the architectural construction of the hall itself. These reproductions aimed to further political projects that used the visibility of global (read imperial) connections in object form to create new national public spheres and ideologies of universal knowledge.

Like casting technologies, photography also emerged in the nineteenth century as an important collecting tool. The vast nineteenth-century photographic archive was drawn upon in the twentieth century to bring new kinds of collections and new types of knowledge into being. One of the most renowned, and provocative, image archives is Aby Warburg's *Mnemosyne* project, which he began in 1927 with the intention of collating a world atlas of images from his archive, now housed in the Warburg Institute in London. Warburg's 'iconology', a 'science of culture' (*Kulturwissenschaft*), his collection and comparative study of the world through images, was closely allied to the nineteenth ethnological imperative of salvage collection that used the process of collecting to inscribe timeless forms of knowledge on what was perceived to be a moment of rapid global transformation.[19]

By the time of Warburg's death in 1929, he had curated 63 black hessian-covered screens upon which were mounted nearly a thousand photographs.[20] This method of display, devised by Warburg's colleague

Figure 25 Aby Warburg, *Picture Atlas Mnemosyne*, 1928–9, Panel 79. © The Warburg Institute. Reproduced with permission.

Fritz Saxl, 'presented an easy way of marshalling the material and reshuffling it in ever new combinations'.[21] Warburg's *Atlas* mapped the movement of enduring icons across time and space, highlighting the recursive psychological elements and motifs within global art forms, captioned with epigrams ('Beneath the dark flutter of the griffon's wings we dream – between gripping and being gripped – the concept of consciousness').[22] Warburg's collection of photographs overcame the boundaries of media, uniting images gleaned from museums, advertising, photography, coins and stamps, making visible a genealogy of images, as they migrated across materials, uniting key forms within art and history.[23] Warburg saw the collating of images as a powerful tracing of (cultural) memory. His project pushed the poetics and the philosophical underpinnings of the picture library into new territory, recognising the collection of images as the foundation for a new kind of knowledge practice and a new way to understand the ways in which images are embedded themselves within the reproduction of human culture.

Another key touchstone for the role of image libraries as museums in their own right is Andre Malraux's *Musée imaginaire* (translated in English as *Museum without Walls)*. This virtual project, published by Malraux in book form, argued for the collation of reproductions as a way to image and imagine new global connections and forms of art historical knowledge in the mind of the viewer.[24] Malraux's understanding of knowledge in his imaginary museum emerges from acts of juxtaposition and analogy, revolving around the visual comparison of photographic images, which transcend the specificities of the original objects they reference. It could be argued that this perspective has been fundamentally internalised in the processes of digitisation, for instance in the online museum catalogues that present all objects in standardised form, focusing on novel methods of connecting and searching among them internalising the algorithmic capacities of digital media to extend the comparative epistemology developed in the archive of image-objects in the nineteenth-century museum.

Design objects in the museum

The decorative art museum brings together an understanding of objects as images, but also as technologies, drawing explicit attention to the ways in which things emerge but are not purely defined by particular materials.[25] From their inception, museums of decorative arts were to inspire the production, and consumption, of objects for everyday life as well as special objects of 'high' or elite culture. Despite, or perhaps because of, the entanglements between the commercial, the industrial and the colonial, museums of decorative art are still developing their commitment to understanding the museum as a place of making and doing, a place in which art and craft come together. For example, the Cooper Hewitt has a 'process lab', which focuses on unpacking the practice of design (rather than the making of objects):

> *Embracing our motto of 'Play Designer,' the Process Lab is a dynamic new way to enjoy the museum and experience the creative process of design firsthand. Here you can participate in design thinking as though you were a designer, by engaging in a series of digital and physical activities based in four categories: getting ideas, prototyping with materials, critiquing, and evaluating everyday design solutions.*[26]

Design is presented as a process of 'thinking' through images towards objects. Digital media, with its recursive constitution of object and image, becomes the perfect form to articulate this vision of making and to enable very specific forms of visitor participation.

Design into the digital

There is a marked continuity between the discussions about design that emerged in museums of decorative arts in the nineteenth and early twentieth centuries and the ways in which twenty-first-century digital technologies are understood to bring together craft, capitalism and design. This latter occurs within a program of accessibility and democratisation achieved through processes of translation and reproduction across different media. While programmes to gather together reproductions and ensure the continued reproduction of museum collections in new design industries made technologies of copying visibly part of museum collections, the digital processes of reproduction are generally presented by museums as supplementary, or outside of the museum collection – as part of the visitor experience, but not as collections in their own right. In turn, the growth of digital production across numerous sectors provides museums with a series of conceptual problems for collecting, curating and conserving.[27] Museums have conventionally struggled with collecting the immaterial, and in the museum context the digital shifts between being a technology that enables the collection and reproduction of new kinds of artefact to being a social tool of accessibility, largely through imaging (and to a lesser extent through the production of other embodied states).[28]

The example of the Victoria and Albert's purchase of a 3D-printed gun, 'The Liberator', by American activist Cody Wilson, part of the museum's new 'rapid response' collecting initiative, works through many of these issues. The debates that emerged around this acquisition, including anxiety about what in fact was being collected, highlighted the complex ways in which digital technologies continue to be effaced or dissolved, even as they constitute new kinds of objects and new regimes of collection and care. The museum questioned whether it should collect the first fired prototype of the gun, or the code that produced it. Legal, customs and ethical constraints meant that the museum eventually printed a version of the gun in the UK, but with certain components printed in plaster so that the printed gun was in fact not useable.[29] For the gun's creator, Cody Wilson, 'The Liberator' was part of a radical libertarian/anarchist challenge to the authority of the state to regulate a citizen's right to bear arms. The 3D print collected by the museum was modified to render it useless, making it a very different kind of object.[30]

The questions raised by these new kinds of replicable objects both depart radically from previous issues concerning reproduction and bring

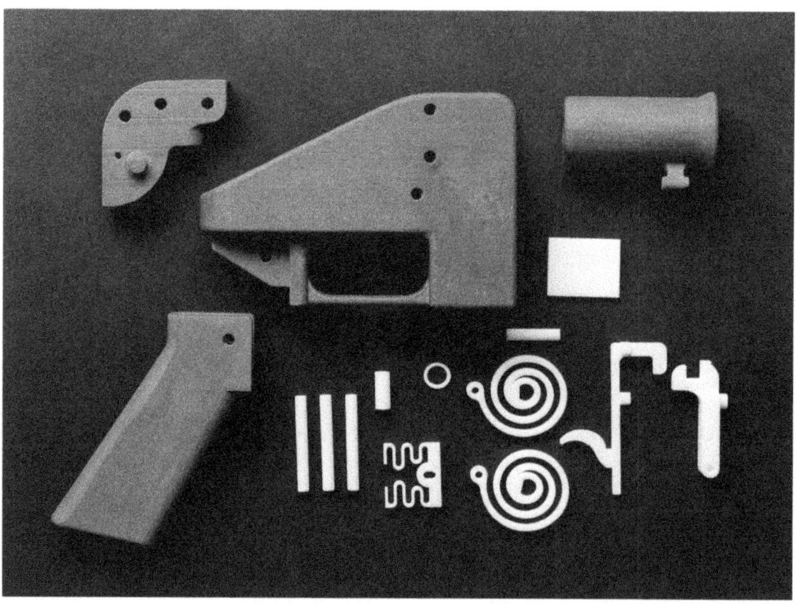

Figure 26 'The Liberator', a 3D-printed handgun, in plaster and plastic, printed by Digits 2 Widgets, manufactured from the CAD designed by Defense Distributed, 2013. CD.1:1 to 16-2013 © Victoria and Albert Museum, London. Reproduced with permission.

new issues to the table. Performance art and conceptual art, alongside photography, video and film have all long provoked conversation in museums about the relationship between the artwork and its documentation, the boundaries of the collected artefacts, the property regimes that underpin the materials used, and the appropriate conditions of care, collection and display.[31] As I have been exploring throughout this book, many of these questions are not in fact new, but are re-emerging as new technologies appear and interact with older forms of collection. Museums are still recognised as platforms for and practices of objectification, stalwarts of materiality, places that fix and freeze the immaterial, the social and the performative in object form.[32] This implies a set of very distinct identities for digital objects in museums, which span the ephemera of documentation or audio-visual supplement through to the conversion of digital projects into a series of new kinds of object forms – valued, perhaps, not for their digital qualities, but for the ways in which they can be translated into museum languages of collection.[33]

The Pen

In 2011, the Cooper Hewitt closed for total renovation in order to rethink the relationship between the opulent Upper East Side mansion within which it was housed and the history and intention of the collection. Technology and media were crucial parts of the re-imagination of the space, with an extravagant budget underpinned by sponsorship from Bloomberg Philanthropy. Alongside expanding the gallery spaces and extending the café, gift shop and education rooms, a newly mediated visitor experience was designed. At the reopening in 2015, visitors experienced several interlocking digital interventions into the space. The house itself was presented through an interactive large-screen multimedia display that allowed the visitor to explore the architectural features and original layout of the house (based on a large-scale and high-resolution three-dimensional scan of the entire building). Similar flat screens, mounted as tables, are positioned throughout the galleries, to be used in conjunction with the Pen as portals into the digitised collection. One table was dedicated to the history of the collections, allowing the visitor to explore which objects were given by whom, and to learn about the background of the museum's founding collectors from high-society New York City. Another table in a small room of its own, 'The Immersion Room', was dedicated to highlighting the wallpaper collection of the institution. Visitors can use the touch-screen table to select wallpaper samples that may be projected onto screens comprising two full walls of the small room, allowing the wallpaper to be seen not just as a swatch but as it would look on a wall. Visitors can also use the Pen to design their own wallpaper, using a simple painting program, and project their own design onto the walls around them.

The touch screens throughout are linked not only to the digital collections but also to the objects on display through the interface of the Pen. The Cooper Hewitt is the only Smithsonian museum to charge admission and this plays into the sense of value for money received by visitors when, upon purchasing a ticket, they are given a smooth, thick black rod, with a

Figure 27 The Immersion Room at the Cooper Hewitt, October 2015. Photograph by Haidy Geismar.

lace to put over the wrist. They are then shown very briefly how to press down the tip of the Pen onto marked cross signs on object labels throughout the gallery. Pressing the Pen onto these marks 'saves' the objects in a virtual collection storage space; these are private and unique to each visitor and, through the creation of an account, can be saved from visit to visit. The saved objects can also be accessed through the tables, where they may be explored in relation to other objects in the collection and linked to objects designed by the visitor themselves. The Pen unites a number of different digital and interactive experiences: The History of the Mansion, the Immersion Room and the Process Lab, as well as the exhibits, collections database and the interactive tables throughout the galleries.

Unlike many museums, more than 90 per cent of the Cooper Hewitt's collection has been digitised and made available online through a searchable web interface.[34] The objects saved through the Pen are not images of the object as seen in the gallery. Instead visitors are taken directly to the digital catalogue entry, which typically presents a disembodied, high-resolution image that can be zoomed into on the table, or at home, allowing them to explore the surface texture of the object. Saved objects can be accessed through a user account and web interface. Here, visitors may add their own comments, and choose if they want to make their collections public, in the process curating their own pathway through the digital database.

Figure 28 Installation view of 'David Adjaye Selects'. Photograph by Allison Hale © 2015 Cooper Hewitt, Smithsonian Design Museum. Reproduced with permission. Source: http://cooperhewitt.photoshelter.com/image/I0000mHenen5iODc.

In an example drawn from one of my visits to the museum in 2015, a textile, selected by architect David Adjaye, hangs in one of the lavish reception rooms from a gilded rail, allowing you to catch the interplay of warp and weft. In the catalogue, however, it appears flatly in two dimensions, losing all sense of its sensuous tactility, its potential to be draped around the body, to be used as cloth (see the chapter in this volume on our attempts to visualise a Māori cloak). We see here the flattening effects of long histories of museum display, the powerful impact they have had on museum processes of visualisation and the way we look at objects in digital space.

The digital design team at the Cooper Hewitt, working with the design company Local Projects, devised five concepts for the digital interface in the galleries: play; social interactive experiences (not just interaction but engagement through interactive devices, e.g. watching others); a discouragement of the app experience (in which visitors

Figure 29 Screengrab of Adire wrapper (Gambia) from the Adjaye exhibition in the collection management system. Reproduced from website under fair use.

spend more time on their personal devices than they do looking at the galleries); extending the visit itself (termed 'persistence of visit'); and allowing for collecting in a scrapbooking-like manner to maintain an ongoing engagement with the museum after the visit.[35] Chan and Cope, leading the Cooper Hewitt digital redesign, explicitly picked up on Ross Parry's definition of a 'post-digital museum', in which Parry argues that digital technologies are now so deeply normalised and embedded within all museum operations that they have ceased to be a distinct category of artefact and practice.[36] As an object lesson in design, the Pen creates a very particular series of experiences of the collection. Indeed, Seb Chan, then Head of Digital at the Cooper Hewitt, has argued that the museum has been reconceptualised around the Pen as a portal into the API drawn from the collections management system. He comments that the 'requirements demanded by the Pen and Pen-related infrastructures impacted every layer of the museum's staff, its physical plant, its budgeting process and its day-to-day operations'.[37]

The Pen, as an object lesson, is a hybrid digital analogue artefact that emphasises the importance of technologies of reproduction in museums. It is explicitly intended by its creators to provide a 'looking up' experience – it is not an app, in which the focus of visitor attention is drawn to the screen of a mobile device. It aims to allow visitors to navigate exhibitions via their own act of collecting. Its materiality – as an object both bulky and light – which within the first week of its launch was working somewhat erratically (in part due to user errors in holding the Pen at the correct angle to the table and for long enough to be able to sync the two and have your collection emerge onto the touch screen), provides a digital interface between the visitor and the collection. It acts as an extension of the museum catalogue – providing the visitor with an alternative way of navigating through the museum database. The Pen ensures that digital media is both used to expand the physical visit and that the visitor's digital collection feeds back into the collections database, ensuring 'that nothing would be held back artificially from the web'.[38] The physical space of the museum therefore becomes an extension of the virtual collection as much as vice versa.

At other points on both the first and second floors, large touch-screen tables allow visitors to upload their collections, look at artefacts from the database and 'design' a series of iconic objects using the Pen or their fingers. The Pen is therefore both a portal into the collections and a tool enabling visitors to look at 'design' and attempt to become the 'designers' of a preordained series of objects (hat, lamp, table, chair, building, wallpaper) in a series of materials (textile, stone, ceramic, metal). Finger and Pen are interchangeable in this design process – both are fairly clumsy instruments with only a limited range. Visitors can draw lines or circles and select from a preordained series of options. A final interface between the Pen/finger and the collection comes from the table itself. Any mark made on the black screen of the table is mapped onto a line within an item from the collection. Circles find circles, and squares, squares. More complex shapes are ironed out into preprogrammed lines that find their correlate from a sample of objects in the database.

The Pen was launched in March 2015, and in the first 75 days the take-up rate was more than 90 per cent across all age ranges and demographics. Visitors collected objects more than 700,000 times, engaging with over 3,600 distinct objects. Some 31 per cent of the visitors went on to create museum accounts, allowing them continued engagement with their collected content.[39] During a conversation I had at one of the digital tables, a Pen user talked explicitly about how he was saving objects to reflect upon back at home as part of his own woodcarving practice, a link that the early collecting initiatives of the Cooper daughters aimed to inspire. But for many people, the Pen effects a simulation or an image of design itself by encouraging a kind of 'design thinking', which here is experienced as something quite different from understanding design as a set of skilled practices.

What then are the object lessons imparted by the Pen? The user experience of the Pen provides an object lesson in values around design, and around a designed visitor experience. For visitors, the instructional video positions the Pen as a collecting tool, which provides an interface between viewers and the table that can also help them to learn and play.[40] The Pen proposes the museum experience be seen as a form of design practice as well as the presentation of a design collection. The Pen is so well established as a mode of engagement with the objects on display that the pristine white labels of the temporary exhibition on the top floor were smudged with black rubber as visitors had attempted to 'collect' and click on object labels, even those not marked as compatible with the requisite cross mark. In this way, the Pen provides an experience of collecting, and continues the trajectory of the decorative arts museums, to underscore the commodity status of design objects.

This digital/analogue interface around the Cooper Hewitt collections continues the trajectory of the decorative arts collection and the photo library in shaping the underlying epistemology of the design museum. The Pen renders objects to be experienced as standardisable, comparable, ahistorical and abstracted. The digital materiality of the combination of Pen and table (and later, at home, the computer screen) renders design as reduced to two dimensions and to the surface of things: style becomes reducible to a graphic linearity. The design process itself is experienced through the opportunities to play on the table. Through this interaction, the collections are experienced through a linear process of recognition, selection and standardisation. Techniques specific to materials are flattened by software – and indeed the object itself is flattened into metadata, the image reduced to standardised motifs and a series of classifications that then link it to other objects. These classifications are both the standard museum classifications of form, time period and function, but they also incorporate the more social aspect of the database. As visitors upload their own comments and categories, they may in the future be included in the searchable metadata for objects.

The digital artefacts in the Cooper Hewitt (tables and pens) therefore allow for a degree of interaction with the very concept of design itself.[41] Design is both presented as a recursive practice between object and image, but also as a mask or cipher, hiding elements of making in favour of a final product or image. Throughout the exhibit, design is framed as a process of formal comparison, of relating through the body of the visitor (and attendant forms of scale). The Pen was developed to be active, reading tagged objects and amalgamating the viewer experience through a recorded pathway in the museum. In this remediating process, the digital image library's efficacy is cast in terms of social networks and of the expansion of the visibility of the collections. However, the focus on the user, and on the creative capacities believed to be inherent within digital technologies, obscures the ways in which the collections management system in fact develops very particular ways of looking at the collection; ways that are embedded in the history of how to see, and do, in the decorative arts museum. The Pen exemplifies the ways in which digital tools are part of broader trajectories of thinking, forms of engagement and engagement with form, tied to historically located genres of collection, exhibition and museological theory. Both the Pen and the box highlight the ways in which digital media must be understood in the broader histories of technologies and techniques of collection and display and in relation to wider forms of classification, knowledge and value that have developed over time and long predate the digital. In the following two chapters I explore the possibilities for rupturing the seamless transition between digital and analogue museologies, exploring the possibilities of digital media to presence multiple forms of knowledge about and within ethnographic collections.

5
Effigy

Essentially, museums have strived to create a world of factual objects almost completely separate from human concerns, desires and conflicts, using systems of classification, acquisition, and documentation procedures.[1]

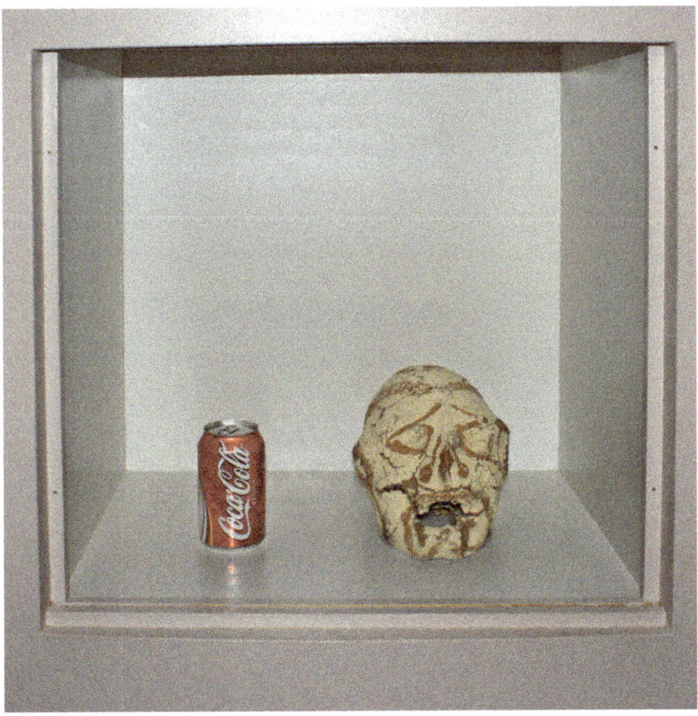

Figure 30 Installation at Mathers Museum of World Cultures, Indiana, with Iatmul overmodelled skull and can of Coca-Cola. Reproduced with permission.

In this chapter, I run down Fifth Avenue, from the Cooper Hewitt to the Metropolitan Museum of Art. Questions of visibility and the entanglement of object and information provoked by the box and the Pen as technologies that envelope collections are also at the forefront of the exhibition of so-called 'non-Western' culture in Euro-American museums: a category that is defined by the detachment of objects from contexts and the making of new contextual knowledge in museums.[2] The complex colonial legacies of the nineteenth century are still present in the ways in which collections from former colonies are often bracketed as 'non-Western'. For example, in March 2015, I was invited to a series of workshops held at a museum of 'world cultures' housed on the campus of an American university. On the first day, our group was given a tour of the recently installed permanent exhibition. The first display to greet us was a glass case set into the wall. In the case was a red can of Coca-Cola and next to it was an overmodelled and decorated skull from the Iatmul area of Papua New Guinea. The effect of this juxtaposition was startling. Several of us were both disturbed and intrigued by the display, which we deduced was intended to demonstrate the tensions between cultural homogeneity and heterogeneity in our perception of world cultures. Those of us who were members of, or worked with, Indigenous communities were used to a more nuanced and careful display of human remains. The attached labels used the same analytic criteria to evaluate both the overmodelled skull and soft drink can, commenting on global knowledge and cultural difference.[3]

This small case emerges from the history of ethnographic display, which has long developed display strategies of juxtaposition and affinity.[4] It teaches far more than it perhaps intended. It is also an object lesson in the ways in which political, ethical and legal concerns concerning the collection and display of human remains are not uniform across contexts, and do not display universally recognised perspectives on globalisation and its colonial legacies. It directs us to appreciate that it is the observer, as much as the curator, who draws these two objects together. If polyphony, collaboration and multiplicity are the hallmark of contemporary museum anthropology, this display underscores how this perspective of multiplicity and difference (the soft drink can and the overmodelled skull) in fact bolsters a worldview that is still disturbingly caught in a series of loops I would describe as primitivist, romantic and colonial. And as this display demonstrates, this is not simply a problem of the nineteenth-century ethnographic museum. Critics noted similar tensions in the permanent displays of the Musée du quai Branly when it opened in Paris in 2007, and in a number of other high-profile museums dedicated to the display of ethnographic collections.[5] Designed by the 'star' architect Jean Nouvel, collections from the former Musée des Colonies (later the Musée des Arts d'Afrique et d'Océanie) and the Musée de l'Homme are displayed at the Musée du quai Branly in labyrinthine pathways, linked together in rooms that turn away from Paris, into the darkness, framed by the rich jungle of the museum's garden.

Nor is this a problem simply of analogue exhibitions – this perspective can also be extended into the digital domain. We could compare this case with new media projects, for instance, a video, part of a recent 'experiment' at the Humboldt Lab. This cutting-edge space is dedicated to exploring issues surrounding ethnographic collections and display, as part of the development of what will be the largest ethnographic museum project in Europe when it opens on Museum Island in Berlin.[6] This particular project uses digital media to explore different subjectivities around collections from the Northwest Coast of America: both a mobile app with which the visitor can tour the collection and a video game. The tour, Totem's Sound, displaces the curatorial authority of the museum by ventriloquising the objects themselves. A disembodied voice, an actor reading from a script, speaks from the subject position of the masks about their Indigenous significance. The video game allows you to inhabit the subject position of colonial collector Johann Adrian Jacobsen as he made his way, in the style of Pac-Man, through Northwest Coast communities, amassing his museum collection.

This digital project may purport to bring 'alternative' voices to the collection, yet like the can of coke and the overmodelled skull in the American museum, they encompass this plurality with a seemingly 'global' perspective, a bird's eye view that in fact naturalises a very particular cultural position. My focus on an effigy from Vanuatu in this chapter explores the ways in which the reality effects of museum objects may be understood as a matter of perspective, and asks what perspectives emerge within digital projects. Digital media are often perceived to be powerful indices of the 'real' world within museum displays, yet this perception of indexicality is carefully crafted through a combination of technological, social and material practices.

The matter of perspective

What perspectives can a single object, an effigy, hold together within the museum? Effigies, perhaps more than any other category of object, complicate the relationship between objects and meaning, especially since their perceived representational status is so often overwritten by the fact that these forms frequently contain human remains, making them indices as well as representations of the human body.[7,8]

Effigies are containers as much as they are depictions of human form and their use in ritual ceremony (from reliquaries in Catholic cathedrals through to funeral effigies in the South Pacific) is to function as changelings between the human and the non-human world.

In the airy glass-walled atrium of the Rockefeller wing at the Metropolitan Museum of Art, which displays objects from the museum's Department of the Arts of Africa, Oceania and the Americas, a small door opens onto a storage space filling the area behind the backs of two parallel display cases. In this invisible storage area stands a rambaramp, a mortuary effigy, from the small island of Tomman, off the southern

Figure 31 Ancestor effigy/rambaramp in storage in the Rockefeller Wing of the Metropolitan Museum of Art. 2000.615. Photograph by Haidy Geismar. © Metropolitan Museum of Art. Reproduced with permission.

coast of Malakula, Vanuatu. Standing on its own in storage, it suggests a starting point – a situated space, out of time, out of context and out of the collection. The object is experienced by those lucky enough to have the keys to the secret storage area as singular. As I was to discover during my research in the museum, this situation reflects not just the seemingly prosaic concerns of the conservation department that the diffused light of the gallery should not diminish the brightness of the pigments painted onto this figure. Rather, it reflects a chasm in the representational fabric of the museum, a clash of worldviews, or perspectives, that problematises the technologies of ethnographic representation and the ways in which the museum uses objects to produce meaning about the world.

> *To whom it may concern: I collected this figure from the now abandoned village of Lik-Lik om Toman [sic] Island in 1969… The effigy was the property of a minor chief known by the name Estel. By his own account the effigy contained the skull and spirit of a close family relative who had in his life risen to some prominence in the tribe. Note the elaborate protuberance rising from the shoulders and the faces on and above the shoulders and on the chest. These signify the position or rank that this person held in the community. According to Estel this man in his life had risen to the ninth grade out of a possible maximum of eleven steps or grades. Almost all of the Rambaramps on Toman Island were destroyed in 1952 when all of the islanders apart from Estel and his immediate family accepted Christianity.*[9]

In museum collections, Malakula is one of the most celebrated islands of Vanuatu, made so by the proliferation of ritual material culture, long collected by museums and documented by anthropologists, linguists and archaeologists.[10] Figures such as the rambaramp, which these collectors adored, and continue to adore, were made to represent named ancestors and spirits, and to link men to rank and titles within a series of public and secret societies through which they pass to consolidate their political, religious, economic and social status. Ritual societies focused on the production of political and spiritual authority are spread across the North Central region of Vanuatu and known in Bislama (the national creole) as *Nimangki* (a term drawn from the local word for these rites in South Malakula). They materialise a political system of male authority, a culture of memorialisation, and a materialisation of ancestral affect that resonates across Melanesia.[11]

Figure 32 Rambaramp in the National Museum of Victoria, Melbourne, No. 3347, from Port Sandwich, Malekula, purchased from Lieutenant W.J. Colquhoun R.N. of HMS *Royalist* in 1890. © University of Cambridge Museum of Archaeology and Anthropology. P.3978. ACH1. Reproduced with permission.

Figure 33 The Melanesia section (Gallery 354) of the Michael C. Rockefeller Wing, Galleries for the Arts of Africa, Oceania and the Americas, the Metropolitan Museum of Art, photographed 2011. New York, Metropolitan Museum of Art. © Metropolitan Museum of Art/Art Resource/Scala, Florence. Reproduced with permission.

In the Melanesia section of the Rockefeller wing, headdresses, masks, figurative drums and carved house posts embodying and representing ancestral spirits and their mobilisation to afford status resonate with Malanggan carvings from New Ireland, Asmat bisj (memorial) poles and hook figures from the Sepik region of Papua New Guinea. Visually, the hall exemplifies the role that sculptural and figurative arts play in bringing the world of the ancestors into the world of the living, facilitating the movement and interconnection between these two worlds. Malanggan, bisj poles and rambaramp are all artefacts that replace human bodies after death with cultural images; in doing so, this facilitates the passage of the human spirit into the world of the ancestral spirits. As these images emerge from behind screens and fences, at the peak of ritual activity, there is a social recognition that this person, in becoming an ancestor, authorises future generations to appropriate and maintain their power and status within their own bodies. These wooden figures do not freeze a person in time and space – they permit the transfer of authority and power across a skin of body and wood. In time, if they have not been collected for a museum or by an art dealer, they will be allowed to rot back into the earth, continuing the cycle of material transference, affecting a surface tension between presence and absence.[12]

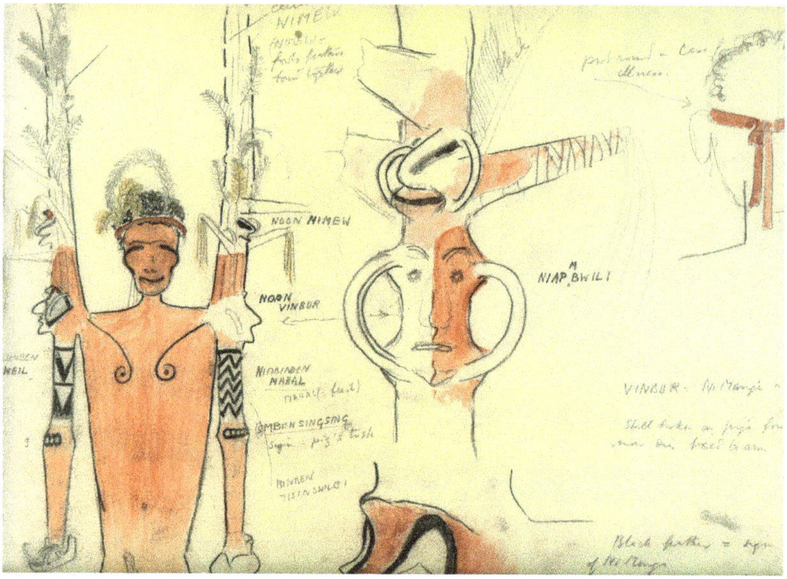

Figure 34 Drawings of a rambaramp in the Sydney Museum by A.B. Deacon, c.1926. Cambridge University Library Special Collections: Haddon Papers 16-014. © Cambridge University Reproduced with permission.

The process of collecting and exhibiting these artefacts together naturalises a number of formal qualities of these artefacts – their ritual function, their mnemonic capacities, and the fact that they should really be seen as complex assemblages or collections in themselves rather than as singular artefacts.

The juxtaposition of these objects within museum displays overwrites the internal juxtapositions within each object in which their material forms (wood, skeletal material, fibre, spider's webs, pigment) work together to create a composite sense of number that in turn provides very specific (magical) reality effects. As such, this multiplicity is generally recognised by museums as singular in form, as Susanne Küchler has observed, a representational context that is 'riddled by the legacy of semiotics and the annihilation of analogy'.[13] The tensions and problems raised by this particular framing of museum collections were made explicit as I explored the files and archives for the rambaramp in the Metropolitan Museum of Art. Working with Oceania curator Maia Nuku, I found an archival discrepancy between two different documents detailing the provenance of the piece.

> ***Q: What was the name of the man it [the rambaramp] commemorated? What was his clan etc?***

A: It is not known who the rambaramp commemorates due to the fact that the skull that makes up this rambaramp was taken from the Solomon Islands by a woman known as Mrs Tesa.[14]

In the account I presented earlier, the dealer who sold the effigy to the American collector who then donated the piece to the Metropolitan Museum describes where he bought the piece, and what he believes it to be: a ritual artefact that forms part of the mortuary traditions of South Malakula, which represents a high-ranking man, indeed containing his spirit and his skull. In the second account, an extract from a recent letter from the director of Vanuatu Cultural Centre paraphrases the answers by a local fieldworker to a series of questions emailed by Eric Kjellgren, the curator of the collection at the Metropolitan Museum at the time. The Vanuatu Cultural Centre, as has been extensively documented, has created a network of volunteer researchers, based in their home community and who act as gateways for cultural research, facilitating external researchers and ensuring that their research is matched to community needs, interests and expectations.[15] The fieldworker from South Malakula, answering the curator's questions, stated that while the rambaramp *was* produced by Asen Maki and depicted designs and iconography authentic to the Nimangki grade-taking system, the piece had been made to order using a skull that had supposedly been brought into Vanuatu from the Solomon Islands. In response to the curator's final question over email, 'Is there anything the people on Tomman would like the visitors to know or think about viewing the rambaramp?', the answer given was: 'They would like other people to respect all of their custom/culture.' During the renovation of the Oceania Hall in 2008, the rambaramp was taken off display. The reason given in the object's dossier was a concern that the natural light that suffuses the hall was potentially damaging to the pigments and natural fibres of the piece, even though it is clearly in better condition (and is younger) than most of the other objects currently on display.

These archival disagreements refract through the body of the rambaramp itself, which remains suggestive of multiple frames of reference. It is both a typical example of a ritual artefact – good enough as an illustration – and an inauthentic commission that would be highly problematic by the ethical standards of today surrounding the collection and display of human remains by museums. From the perspective of the people of Vanuatu, the images on the body of the effigy are 'real', the identity of the person is (possibly, probably) falsified. From the perspective of the collector and dealer, the object is part of a complex, radically different, ritual tradition containing a 'real' Melanesian. Can we manage such an inversion of the turn in museology to prioritise the native perspective? What happens when the native perspective is more rational, better historicised and clearer than the analytic perspective of the Euro-American art market, which here is seen as smudged at best, corrupt at worst? Can we escape from the inevitable presentation of multiple perspectives that 'frame' objects in museums? Is one perspective always more powerful?[16]

Much contemporary museum practice is still dedicated to keeping these interpretive spheres apart, privileging single over multiple perspectives. In 2008, the same year that the Rockefeller wing was reinstalled, the Metropolitan Museum of Art was compelled by law to return to Italy the Euphronios Krater, a celebrated painted vase by the Ancient Greek artist Euphronios that was found to have been illegally exported and which had been in the museum's collections since 1971. As part of the protracted legal proceedings and subsequent negotiations, the Italian government agreed to loan, for the duration of four years per work, several other antiquities as a kind of 'compensation' to the museum for the loss of one of the most significant objects within its Greek and Roman collections (notwithstanding the fact that the legal investigation uncovered that the museum had more than likely known that the piece had been illegally excavated and exported).[17] The labels of these objects in the galleries, agreed to be of 'equivalent beauty and importance', simply say that they are on long-term loan from the Republic of Italy. How important are the histories of collection and display to the 'real' meaning and social significance of these objects? How much of the context can be contained in the form of the object itself?

Juxtaposition and perspectivism

Museums have historically held together multiplicity within a singular world, inflected by the dominant values and modes of looking, which Tony Bennett has termed an 'exhibitionary complex', a way of looking, historically located in the Euro-American nation-state.[18] In recent years, a lively branch of anthropology has emerged that attempts to develop long-standing concerns within the discipline regarding difference, translation and knowledge across cultures. The so-called 'ontological turn' links philosophy and anthropology to challenge the notion of cultural

Figure 35 The Euphronois Krater on display during its final days at the Metropolitan Museum of Art, 11 January 2008. Photograph by Ross Day. Reproduced with permission.

Figure 36 Journalists and authorities view the Euphronios Krater vase during a news conference in Rome, 18 January 2008. Photograph by Dario Pignatelli. © Reuters/Dario Pignatelli. Reproduced with permission.

relativism.[19] In the introduction to a volume focused on understanding objects across cultural contexts, Henare, Holbraad and Wastell argue against the relativist position that we need to understand objects as having meaning within specific worldviews. They argue against a multiculturalist perspective in which each person or culture has its own interpretation of a particular artefact, drawing on the work of Eduardo Viveiros de Castro to advocate a move from 'perspectivalism' (the drawing together of different perspectives) to 'perspectivism', inspired by the Nietzschean view of multiple conceptual schemes that reflect not simply different epistemologies, but ontologies. Rather than focusing on multiple perspectives within a single world, they suggest we should focus on multiple worlds (or acknowledge the possibility of radically different worlds).[20] It seems to me that museums fundamentally confound this academic argument about ontological difference. The political tensions around the presentation of singularity in museums and the tension between the eradication and celebration of polyphony speak to a complex continent that cannot be divided. As the case of the rambaramp shows, multiple perspectives exist on many levels within this singular artefact. It makes no sense to purify the rambaramp into singular worlds, nor to settle for multiple worldviews in order to interpret it, when these meanings are situated so firmly within the object itself (the skull of dubious provenance, the marks and insignia, the social role of the object in both museum and community).

Andrew Moutu, curator of the National Museum of Papua New Guinea, has argued for a perspective on collections that he draws from his own fieldwork as an Arapash man working among the Iatmul people. In his view, knowledge is built up, not from the organisation of objects according to an overarching narrative (exemplified, for instance, by the idea of the Pitt Rivers Museum's typological approach to display) but through what Moutu describes as 'juxtaposing analogies', bringing things together in creative and generative ways.[21] It could be argued that this is a particularly Melanesian sensibility of understanding not just objects but the very process of interpretation itself.

The rambaramp, as it stands in the Metropolitan Museum of Art, holds multiple perspectives together in the form of an artefact that is conceptually multiple rather than singular, unravelling the need to determine authentic, singular truth or truths. This multiplicity is evoked in both the Indigenous exegesis in which rambaramps hold together the world of the living and the dead, the collective world of the ancestral authority, and the memory of an individual person. It is also evoked in the interpretive tensions raised by the multiple provenances and histories presented within its archival record, which construct our understandings of its authenticity and historicity in the art world. The multiple perspectives contained within this object cannot be divorced from each other. In fact, they produce one another. Their intimate entanglements demonstrate not a clash in worldviews, or the existence of incommensurable worlds, but rather an onion skin of interdependent contexts.

Into the digital

These examples seem to support an analytical position in which we look at singular objects, around which swarm multiple perspectives, or interpretive positions that change according to the ethical, political and cultural frameworks that inflect museum displays. The rambaramp can be a ritual artefact, or a copy made for the market. We can see the Euphronios Krater as Italian, or as part of a universal global heritage; as art or as loot. The museum itself, as an assemblage of curatorial authority, collections history and exhibitionary technologies, brings these meanings together in very particular ways through the creation of particular subject positions.[22] But what I have started to suggest through my focus on this rambaramp is that objects intervene in their own meanings in important ways, creating perspectives that emerge from material vantage points, as well as those of the museum visitor or curator. The translation of objects into digital form is a moment at which this might be made explicit, although it is too often hidden from sight in the black-boxing of digital mediation. Following Caroline Wright, we might ask at what point does the material form of an object decompose into the systems of value and knowledge that give it meaning? In digital terms, these questions might translate into asking how important is the metadata to the object? Or where does the object itself sit in the clustering of information that constitutes digital representations?

As material forms, objects such as the rambaramp can give us an interesting perspective on the digital remediation of museum collections as they are produced specifically to inspire an understanding of an ongoing process of materialisation and dematerialisation that constructs human culture and society.[23] But how does this understanding of the rambaramp, a purist interpretation that focuses on the Indigenous meaning and resonance of these artefacts, an account that is reinforced within the display labels in museums from New York to Paris, mesh with an account that understands these artefacts as being dynamic players within the global relations of collecting, as part of social processes of interpretation that are strategic and work to promote some perspectives over others? How do these objects interact with the emergent global ethics and forms of governmentality that regulate their production, circulation, display and care? This conundrum, commonplace in our interpretive dilemmas around museum collections, also has the power to inform our understanding of the conceptual toolkit that we use to understand the value, resonance, permanence and even ontology of digital objects. Do digital technologies simply facilitate the conversion of data from one form into another, or do they import specific cultural forms into this process? Articulations of the 'network society' and the political activism of the free and open source software movement highlight the entanglements between code and law and the ways in which code has the capacity to structure specific kinds of social, political and economic operations.[24] For open source coders and theorists, free software produces other kinds of liberty (the freedom to fully utilise software, the freedom to improve upon it and the freedom to understand it) as well as producing social formations that writers such as Chris Kelty have referred to as 'recursive publics': public spheres that are brought into being through the particular ways in which code can combine the social, technical and political in its very form.[25]

In my own work exploring the capacities of digital collections management systems to internalise alternative knowledge systems, I have focused on the tensions between the capacities of digital technologies to both render difference legible and to constitute a 'neutral' platform for the encoding of difference.[26] Indigenous software projects in places such as Australia (e.g. Ara Iritija) and North America (e.g. Mukurtu – a US/Australian Aboriginal collaboration) explicitly attempt to 'decolonise the database' by inscribing Indigenous protocols into the form of the platform, not merely its content, replacing core classificatory schemes imported from colonial knowledge systems with local, Indigenous principles and protocols.[27] Paradoxically, however, these internal reorderings of software platforms reify the ordering logics of the relational database in which everything can be flattened into networks as much as they do Indigenous knowledge systems. In turn, the management of these platforms continues to replicate some of the existing tensions and inequalities produced between curators (or technologists), visitors (the general public) and source community stakeholders.[28]

The fact that collections management systems, and the digital objects within them, have the capacity to be networked, hyperlinked and multisensorial is often obscured within the conventional ways in which they are used in museums. The facility of comparison within the relational database, the capacity of the hyperlink to create multiple pathways emanating from any one place within a knowledge architecture, or the facilities of metadata to embed multiple forms of knowledge within the same object are often muted in these digital projects. It is striking how the singular narratives and perspectives that have historically developed in museums are imported into digital projects. This is evident, for instance, in the online collections presence for the rambaramp in the Metropolitan Museum of Art.[29] A search through the 'collections' engine provides the catalogue entry, detail on the provenance:

Beneath the image and catalogue data of the rambaramp in the website are links to a series of 'related objects', all of which are on view in Gallery 354: a helmet mask from Malakula, a slit gong drum from Ambrym, a bark ornament from Malakula and two tree fern effigies from Ambrym, mimicking the display of ritual culture that one experiences in the hall.

Ancestor Effigy (Rambaramp)

Artist:	Asen Maki
Date:	early to mid-1960s
Geography:	Vanuatu, Tomman Island, Vatbuyang village
Culture:	Tomman Island
Medium:	Human skull, vegetable fiber, bamboo, pig tusks, shell, leaves, fiber, paint
Dimensions:	H. 89 x W. 38 x D. 15 in. (226.1 x 96.5 x 38.1 cm)
Classification:	Basketry-Sculpture
Credit Line:	Gift of Ms. Terry Beck, 2000
Accession Number:	2000.615

Not on view

Provenance

Chief Estel, Malakula,Toman Island, Vanuatu, until 1969; John Fowler, collected Vanuatu, in 1969; Terry Beck, West Hollywood, CA, until 2000

Timeline of Art History (2000-present)

Timelines
Melanesia, 1900 A.D.–present

Figure 37 Screengrab of the rambaramp catalogue entry on the Metropolitan Museum of Art website, 1 March 2016. Provenance given: Chief Estel, Malakula, Toman Island, Vanuatu, until 1969; John Fowler, collected Vanuatu, in 1969; Terry Beck, West Hollywood, CA, until 2000. Source: https://www.metmuseum.org/art/collection/search/318742, last accessed January 15, 2018. Portion reproduced under fair use.

Here, the museum makes visible a particular perspective on the rambaramp, hiding the uncertainties contained in its own archive. The museum's commitment to narrative is exemplified not just in the physical layout of the institution but in the website, which locates many of the artefacts with an online presence within the 'Heilbrunn Timeline of Art History'. Just as one moves within the museum site from Ancient Greece to the Arts of Africa, Oceania and the Americas, highlighting the timeless cultural inheritance of modern art (on the other side of the African galleries), so the website makes 'sense' of the collections by imposing them in a linear narrative that compresses geography and history, place and time into a narrative of linear historicity or progress.

Ross Wilson argues that one might read a museum website as a form of intertextual dialogue with the physical site of the institution. Drawing on critical code studies and digital heritage studies, he uses as an example the website for a British Museum exhibition on Ancient Egypt to argue for an 'analogous relationship between the practices of the museum and the markup and programme languages'.[30] This analogy is less straightforward than a simple translation of one knowledge system (curatorial knowledge) into another (computer code). Wilson demonstrates how the relationship between museum and visitor at the British Museum is increasingly structured as a commercial relation. He shows that this is effected by the use of a commercial search engine developed by Amazon to structure the visitor experience and create connections between objects in the website that focus on forging a relationship between like objects, targeting properties that might resonate in an Amazon search (e.g. visual qualities, visitor interaction and so forth), and structuring a visitor identity as analogous to that of a consumer in an online marketplace.[31]

It seems that digital systems often become analogues of their non-digital counterparts – mapping, and replicating, older representational frameworks, overwriting the capacity of the digital for radical transformation, connectivity and multiplicity with the representation of singular, teleological, narratives. What we see in many digital representations of museum collections is in fact the opposite of digital utopian discourses – museum catalogues, Google flythroughs and websites that enshrine the same issues of classification, narration, value and perspective that are on display in the galleries, and which have been on display for decades, if not hundreds, of years.

So, what might a digital system in New York look like when read through the lens of a complex ritual system in Malakula? The argument of Bowker and Star, and many others, is that classificatory systems produce, as much as they arrange, knowledge of the world.[32] However, one of the reasons that the ritual systems of Vanuatu and other parts of Melanesia continue to confound is in part due to their resistance to such techniques of classification.[33] The systems of status-alteration, evoked through the imagery in this rambaramp, track the social life and political authority of men and women through images, figurative (and non-figurative) forms and names that are continually fracturing and reassembling, referencing different and multiple codes of conduct and political economies. Ethnographers have found these systems notoriously hard to document, even as their efforts have become the latest way in which rank and grades are authenticated.[34] Within these systems, objects, people and political systems are inherently multiple.

What are the possible implications of this for museum systems of display and representation? The stakes are high. If we return to the beginning – the encounter between the overmodelled skull and the can of coke, the visitor and the human other on display – and the ethical tensions and political inequities of representation that underscore this encounter, then we need to think about how a more expanded interpretive field alters and influences our perceptions about the proper perspective to take on these objects. Robin Boast and Jim Enote have raised a trenchant criticism of the ways in which museums have constructed the practice of 'virtual repatriation' (a term often used to refer to the return to communities of digital and digitised collections). They argue that 'digital objects do not represent anything … but gain roles and capacities in their use in different social settings'.[35] For Boast and Enote, digital collections are new material forms rather than simply being representations of old collections. They may reference older collections, but they should not stand in for them in their entirety. Boast and Enote challenge the indexicality, constructed through the techniques of simulation, that are increasingly built into digital visualisations of museum collections, arguing that these need to be understood as new kinds of collections.

Ways of seeing: from the rambaramp to Google Earth

The field of complexity evoked by understanding the rambaramp in both local and global terms may help us to understand the possibilities (and limitations) of digital objects. As the Web presentation of the rambaramp demonstrates, the effigy continues to be framed by structures of museum knowledge that map 'art historical' knowledge across time and space and search for points of singularity to anchor the significance of the piece. Yet these perspectives are inculcated not just in the information that is juxtaposed with objects, but in the very ways in which we are made to look at the objects themselves.

In trying to think this through, I started to explore the ways in which the human skulls had been rendered digitally, to explore the indexicality of effigies in the digital space, and to see how this remediation might shift the sense of perspective that underpins the traditional mode of looking at objects in museums. Perhaps not surprisingly, in wandering the Web, I came to the complex assemblage of people and artefacts that make up Hans Holbein's *The Ambassadors* (1533), a canonical painting within the European tradition of art and art history. *The Ambassadors* is a portrait of two wealthy merchants, surrounded by objects that symbolise both their place in the world and their worldview. It might be argued that the painting works a little like a rambaramp in that it highlights the mutually constitutive relationship between these individuals and the social order

Figure 38 Hans Holbein the Younger, Jean de Dinteville and Georges de Selve (*The Ambassadors*), 1533. Oil on oak. © The National Gallery, London.

that surrounds them. And, like the rambaramp, the painting challenges our perspective through the intervention of a hidden human form that reminds us to think carefully about the pictorial perspectives we, as viewers, are implicated within.

Holbein's painting is renowned for its depiction of an anamorphic skull foregrounded, yet strangely apart from, the subjects of the painting. Holbein's perspectival slippage ('the skull is only visible when the rest of the painting is not', according to the promotional video by the National Gallery) draws our attention to the artifice of painting as a window onto the real.[36] Digital images of *The Ambassadors* highlight these tensions, perhaps unwittingly, but strangely work against the painting, foreclosing the perspective that is necessary in order to 'see' the skull. The version of the painting accessible through the *Google Art Project*, for instance, renders the skull impossible to view. Despite cultivating an aesthetic or impression of freedom and mobility in the gallery, the subject position of the visitor is set. One cannot move around the painting or around the space – it is impossible to look at the painting askance. Despite the capacity of Google's Street View to allow one to create a user pathway, our perception of freely moving through real space is in fact vastly limited to the fixed view of both the Google camera and the design of the platform.

Figure 39 Screengrab view of *The Ambassadors*. Screengrab taken from the *Google Art Project*, October 2016. https://www.google.com/culturalinstitute/beta/asset/the-ambassadors/bQEWbLB26MG1LA.

Figure 40 Screengrab of 100% zoom Gigapixel view of the skull in *The Ambassadors*, from *Google Art Project*, October 2016. https://www.google.com/culturalinstitute/beta/asset/the-ambassadors/bQEWbLB26MG1LA.

The Ambassadors was chosen in the collaboration between the National Gallery and Google as one of the select masterworks to be scanned to extra-high resolution. Instead of only being able to move around the painting in a simulation of the gallery space, the viewer is now able to zoom in to the micro-level – to examine the pigment and brushstrokes that comprise the image. This provides us with a completely different perspective on the painting from how it was painted to be seen (from a distance, but also at an angle). Unlike the contortions necessary to view the anamorphic skull correctly, the Google perspective is not scaled to the human body or dependent on bodily movement. Rather, it provides the viewer with the capacity to see like a machine – in this case a microscope. This can be seen to be taking the drive towards single points of meaning to its most logical conclusion – moving us very literally away from the relativist understandings of perspectives that Holbein was presenting towards the naturalisation of a singular subject position, one located deep within the object itself.

Web presentations of these kind of complex images and artefacts frustrate the viewer, making us overtly aware of how much we need to be trained to see as others do in order to interpret what we see.[37] As the *Google Art Project* shows us, the 'period eye' of the digital is all too often fixed, a kind of automated panopticon controlling the perspective of the viewer. Once I started looking, it became clear that the cutting edge in digital imaging and visualisation in fact remains fixed in what Heidegger has termed 'the age of the world picture' – in which mastery of the world is effected through the technologies of image-making: cartography, lithography and now electromagnetic resonance imaging, laser scanning and photogrammetry.[38] The *Google Art Project* displays two primary modes of looking: a cartographic perspective on images that places them at a certain distance, allowing for the creation of a singular image, and an interiorised view from within the object, giving a singular perspective on the image's material composition.

In another recent exhibition, this time at the British Museum, *Ancient Lives, New Discoveries* highlighted the contributions of digital imaging to the knowledge of museum collections. CT scans were presented of eight mummies from Egypt and the Sudan, ranging from 3500 BC to 700 AD.[39] Instead of actually unwrapping the mummies, CT and other scanning technology was used to look inside both the sarcophagi and the textile wrappings of the bodies, to uncover the bones and flesh within and to create new three-dimensional visualisations. The exhibition displayed the wrapped figures alongside interactive screens that allowed the visitor to peel back the layers, ostensibly to see into the very heart of the mummy. Each of the eight figures was presented as a named person, with a forensic-style dossier describing their appearance and any known health issues, their height, date of living and some basic facts that were put together, largely from inscriptions on their coffins.

Neil MacGregor, then the director of the museum, is quoted on the exhibition press release as saying: 'This new technology is truly groundbreaking, allowing us to reconstruct and understand the lives of these eight, very different, individuals.' While the interactive screens are effective in demonstrating the deftness of CT scanning in terms of looking without disturbing the fabric and wrappings, the assertion that these are new forms of knowing these mummies as people was, to me, jarring. With each mummy, careful discussion of the lavish care and attention paid to the wrappings, and to the carving and painting, often with gold leaf, on the sarcophagus spoke to the esteem with which these figures were held and to their unique qualities as individuals. The exhibition text explained how important the stylised presentation of the cultural, carved body was in mediating both the memory and status of the person in their own present, and in ushering them into the world of the dead, where amulets and small carvings facilitated their comfortable passage. As interesting as it was to look through the digital visualisations at the painstaking ways in which the bodily organs and brains were stored within the skeletal frame, the painting of fingernails and toenails with gold and the scattering of gold leaf within the wrappings, we learn little more of real significance about these people than we already know from the embarrassment of riches within which they were wrapped and contained.

I visited the exhibition with my six-year-old daughter and we were very struck by the figure of Tjayasetimu, a young temple singer, who was probably seven years old when she died in 800 BC. 'Why did she die?' my daughter asked. Despite entering the intimacy of Tjayasetimu's shroud and scanning her body, we do not know. We know more about her humanity from her magnificent coffin. Most tellingly, unlike other mummies, whose carved hands are presented as wrapped within their funeral clothes, Tjayasetimu, Singer of the Interior of Amun, is presented as though she were still alive, with her hands free of her shroud. This more than anything suggested to me a sadness at the death of a child, almost 3,000 years ago. The presentation of these mummies as bones, flesh, brains and organs cannot make them more into individuals then those who crafted their memorials. Indeed, that act of humanity, to protect and preserve these bodies for an infinite future, was what was stripped away by using technologies to peek inside. Like mummies, rambaramps are also curated people – they link rank and title to the human body; social status to life history; people to categories. Like the Google pixelation of *The Ambassadors*, looking beyond the surface of the image gives

Figure 41 Publicity shot from the exhibition *Ancient Lives, New Discoveries*. © The Trustees of the British Museum. Reproduced with permission.

us no 'cultural' information indigenous to the artefact – rather, it exposes a culture of viewing in which the viewer is assumed to be an all-seeing analyst, supposedly able to strip back culture towards a 'pure' engagement with materials.

To return to the rambaramp, it was hard not to 'take sides' during the process of researching the true meaning of the effigy. Can we still primarily view this as an exemplar of a now-lost mortuary tradition? Or should we think of this as a fake, constructed out of illegally collected human remains? This rambaramp contains many paradoxes: it was created as a museum piece in order to be presented as an embodiment of, and an embodied, ritual tradition. The conditions of its production (commissioned by an expatriate who worked for the colonial government) were to produce a subject that could then be presented as part of a pre-colonial, pre-Christian world. The very discourse of multiple perspectives creates an analytical vantage point from which multiple perspectives can be recognised but which depends upon the subject position of the disengaged, impartial observer, or museum visitor. This brings only confusion. Far better for the subject to be the rambaramp itself, which holds this complexity together much more effectively.

Instead of embracing this multiplicity, museum technologies seem to continue to struggle to fix meaning in points of singularity. The rambaramp sits in storage waiting. After a presentation of my research at the Metropolitan Museum, where Maia Nuku and I became excited at the possibilities these multiple stories might have for future displays, the head curator suggested quietly to us afterwards that they might instead think about deaccessioning this piece. For her, we had pushed the rambaramp into an impossible interpretive, and ethical, space.

I have juxtaposed the rambaramp with a number of other projects to image human effigies in digital space in order to complicate the assumptions about both visual knowledge and the nature of perspective that are inbuilt to museum techniques of display. Digital projects, with their sleek and novel interfaces, often obscure the ways in which imaging techniques can encode very particular kinds of imagination. The so-called ontological turn is, for me, nothing like a rambaramp. It relies upon a 'world picture' in order to theorise multiple perspectives from a singular point of analysis. Rambaramps can do something very different. They create a shifting site of meaning that temporally compresses the past and the present, and links classificatory systems (names, ranks), material forms (insignia, images), in a material palimpsest of historicity both fixed and dynamic. This is multiplicity from within, and speaks to a capacity that is also inherent within digital media to remediate, reposition and reconnect. This capacity is unrealised within the current digital mediations of the rambaramp that magnify the structure and values of the museum perspective at the expense of any other. In the following chapter I present a series of more experimental frames for the digitisation of cultural collections in order to demonstrate the possibilities of digital media to open up, rather than foreclose, multiplicity and alternative perspectives.

6
Cloak[1]

We swoop now from New York back to London. In a drawer underneath the shelf that holds empty lantern-slide boxes (one of which was disappeared by Caroline Wright in the *Sawdust and Threads* project) is a beautiful cloak, wrapped carefully in acid-free tissue paper. Here, I detail a project, *Te Ara Wairua*, which attempted to enfold and engage the cloak in numerous digital projects to convert, translate and communicate the form of the cloak using digital media. Unlike the digital formulations of the rambaramp, our experiments in digitisation were exploratory, speculative and at times unsuccessful. We learned from our mistakes to challenge our assumptions about what kind of cultural objects digital media may produce.

Figure 42 *Tukutuku Roimata*, 1.0013 Oceania/New Zealand. Flax, dog hair, wool. Photograph by Stuart Laidlaw. © UCL. Reproduced under a CC-BY-NC-NC 2.0 license.

In the nineteenth-century museum world in which the cloak was collected, objects were the building blocks of knowledge systems that in the twentieth century were decomposed into texts, signs and symbols. This interactive shift transformed objects from being understood as material beings in the world to communicative media, their materiality dissolved into broader systems of signification.[2] This textual logic formed the framework for numerous other ways in which to understand objects: as biographies, narratives and signs.[3] The influence of semiotics, structuralism and theories of communication have contributed to a dominant understanding of digital media as information. The cloak, as she emerged from its drawer into a variety of digital projects, has asked us how we might rethink the boundaries between objects and information or data in the context of digital museum projects. *Te Ara Wairua* was developed with many of these questions in mind, and also brought together concerns about the cultural nature of the digital, the materiality of the digital, and an ethnographic exploration regarding our expectations of how the digital 'works'. Fundamentally, the project explored the slippages between utopian discourses of connection, digital mediation and the ways in which we define and use digital objects. It tracked the realities of social relations as they are inflected through digital objects, mediated through screens, through software platforms and through the realities of cellular and broadband connections.

The project was a collaboration between myself, Stuart Foster and Kura Puke of Massey University and Te Matahiapo Indigenous Research Organization, based in Taranaki, Aotearoa New Zealand. *Te Ara Wairua* is a Māori term meaning 'pathways of spiritual or intangible energy', which we drew around, and through, our Māori cloak. Originally collected by the Wellcome Institute, she came to UCL in the mid-twentieth century. Marked only as 'Māori', she has no known provenance. We do not know who made her, where or when.[4] We do know that she is a special *taonga*, a Māori treasure, and possibly because of her small size made for a child. The cloak is finely woven of New Zealand *harikeke*, or flax, with tassels of hair from the Polynesian dog (*kuri*) and a wool fringe bordering the beautiful red, black and white *taniko* (woven border). The condition of the cloak shows us that she was worn carefully and sparingly, and that it is unlikely much has been done with her since she has been in the UK.

She was brought out of storage in 2013 during a collaborative project between UCL anthropologists and artists working in the School of Material and Visual Culture at Massey University in Wellington, New Zealand. During a preliminary Skype conversation, Māori artist Kura Puke was intrigued by my characterisation of our collection as comprising many 'orphaned' objects, without context or history. Discovering the cloak through her survey of all the Māori objects in our collection, Kura decided to use her research methods and artistic practice – connecting to communities and to Māori knowledge through the creation of immersive digital sound and light installations – to (re)create a provenance for the cloak and to reactivate the spiritual pathways, or *wairua*, that all Māori *taonga* instantiate. Working with another Massey researcher, a spatial and interaction designer, Stuart Foster, we embarked on a year-long exploration of the capacities of digital technologies to encode Māori values, to extend community to the cloak and to imagine her within new representational and relational frameworks. Together we have explored multiple forms of digital materialities and engagements with the object, the status of the cloak as both object and information, and the discourses of the digital and the social that the project has brought together.

During the project, we experimented with three primary digital frames. We constructed an immersive environment in which we used broadband and cellular connections, iPads and platforms such as FaceTime and Skype to bring people in New Zealand into direct engagement with the cloak and with people at UCL. This transnational social space also hosted an experimental virtual environment in which light and sound from New Zealand was processed through a DIY, open source interface that converted sound into lights (through LED) and back into sound, drawing attention to the shared substance of meaning, affect and intentionality that underpinned the different digital media. Finally, we explored the capacities of 3D imaging to create a virtual or digital surrogate of the cloak, with the intention that this data could recirculate back into New Zealand (the next stage of our project). Seeing the digital not as a reified object but as an assemblage that works in the world is crucial to understanding the epistemology, effects and affects of digitised museum collections.

A virtual *powhiri*

With a background in designing virtual environments and a long-standing practice of connecting through light and sound to Māori *taonga*, Kura and Stuart's intention was to 'bring the UCL cloak into the light'. Working closely with the Taranaki-based Te Matahiapo Indigenous Research Organization, they wanted to connect the cloak to a living Māori community. Māori people are renowned for the ways in which they are able to use Indigenous epistemologies and cosmologies to encircle those brought in through the process of settler-colonialism.[5] Categories such as *taonga* encircle that of collection, *kaitiaki* (guardianship) encircles the role of curator, *kaupapa* is used to refer to a correct and wise method of organising research. These terms are increasingly passing into

New Zealand English.[6] They signify not just a kind of translation but also a successful way of making analogies. The process of analogy has been successful and efficacious to register some parts of the radio spectrum and new genetic patents as both *taonga* and as Indigenous intellectual and cultural property. Throughout our project, in conjunction with Te Matahiapo, the term *wairua*, spiritual energy, has been used as both a synonym and an encompassing term for the digital. Just as the digital exists in waves of information, transmitted all around us, so too do *taonga* create networks of connectivity, across both space and time. The connection of this cloak, through broadband and cellular activity, to people in both London and New Zealand was therefore framed not as something new, but as a continuation of the kind of work that *taonga* are supposed to do – to link people, activate and maintain connections and networks of knowledge and sociality. However, in Māori philosophy, knowledge does not simply float freely, it is emplaced in a cosmological cartography called *whakapapa* (often translated as genealogy, used to describe the webs of relationships within which everyone and everything is situated). The lack of conventional provenance of this cloak, and the seeming impossibility (at the present time) of finding her original makers and owners opened up the opportunity to work on a renewal and regeneration of her *whakapapa* and also presented an analytic point of negotiation with the capacity of Indigenous cosmologies to encircle other concepts.

Having worked remotely with me, through Skype, for over a year, Kura and Stuart came to England to activate the project in June 2014. On

Figure 43 *Te Ara Wairua* in the Octagon Gallery at UCL, 17 June 2014. Photograph by Charlie Mackay. Reproduced with permission.

17 June, we created a ceremonial environment in UCL's Octagon Gallery. The gallery was transformed into a Māori ceremonial space, a *marae*, and in the gallery we were welcomed into their space by Dr Te Huirangi Eruera Waikerepuru, Mereiwa Broughton, Te Urutahi Waikerepuru, Tengaruru Wineera, who were at the Te Matahiapo Indigenous Research Organization, in the Wharenui Te Ururongo, Pouakai, at the foot of Mount Taranaki on the North Island of New Zealand. Guests, representatives of UCL Anthropology, Museums and Collections, and members of Ngāti Rānana, the London Māori Club, were ushered in by a *reo po'hiri* or call, into the space, to stand before the cloak, and before the elders who then spoke with chants (*karakia*) and song (*waiata*) to us. Instead of the traditional *hongi*, the sharing of breath, we breathed onto a gift (*koha*), a woven basket from Vanuatu, which was returned eventually to Taranaki.

The event contained the usual tensions that activate any ritual and make it crackle with social energy as we took ancient customs and improvised in new environments and using new tools. Ngāti Rānana, a collective of Māori living in the diaspora, were nervous of their reputation back home and felt that they did not have someone with sufficient status to be able to speak for our side. They also felt that without someone with the appropriate status to *karakia*, they were unable to *waiata*. For much of the event, while we could be heard perfectly in New Zealand, we were unable to hear all of the words of the chant, as they were using a weak cellular rather than broadband connection. This resulted in an experience of unequal reception,

Figure 44 Te Matahiapo in Taranaki, New Plymouth, 17 June 2014, welcoming us from Taranaki onto their *marae*. Photograph by Pip Guthrie. Reproduced with permission.

Figure 45 Representatives of Ngāti Rānana and UCL Museums/Anthropology in the Octagon Gallery. Photograph by Charlie Mackay. Reproduced with permission.

and heightened my perception that digital communications media were layered imperfectly onto the imagined space of social and ritual connection.

We discussed all of this later. While I worried that the problems with sound and reception meant that the efficacy of the ritual was diminished, Kura and Stuart disagreed from very different perspectives. For Stuart, this was simply a technological problem that would eventually be solved. The *principles* of perfect digital connection were there and the ideal of the seamless integration of virtual and real environments was within reach. For Kura, the intention, or spirit, of the ritual was more important than the perfection of its form – as long as there was consensus on what was supposed to happen, and agreement about how it should happen, things could not 'go wrong'. Both Kura and Stuart subsumed the complex materiality of these moments into idealised imaginaries of the project, and both mapped *Te Ara Wairua*, pathways of intangible energy, onto the energetic pathways of digital communications media. I, however, tried to stay true to my own experience: one fraught with anxiety about the digital connection and its implication for our social relations, and also coloured by my own preoccupation about how technology, and rituals, were supposed to 'work'.[7] I wondered if there was even more significance to the lack of sound, or the stilting quality of the connection as we experienced it from our end. As an interaction designer, Stuart started from the assumption that the technology in this project should be invisible, allowing us the perception of an unmediated connection between London and Taranaki. He talked a great deal about the disappearance of technology, and the logic of the project assumed that technology would overwrite the history of this cloak that had placed it thousands of miles away from its communities of origin. As the project progressed and technology increasingly frustrated our attempts to communicate clearly and provide a full audio-visual encounter on both ends we started to talk more and more about what we could learn from what wasn't working perfectly. I wondered often how we could overwrite a history that inscribed anonymity onto the diaspora that was also an important part of the cloak's identity. I asked how we might digitally and ritually evoke the situation in London that provided an important context for the cloak in the present day. At one point we recorded the sounds of the Euston Road and of foxes in my back garden (some speculate that the call of the fox is similar to that of the Polynesian dog) in order to add them to our databank of material for our proposed virtual experience of the cloak.

Perhaps the 'failings' of technology at the *powhiri*, and the ways in which it kept reminding us of its presence, evoked exactly the situation we were in – a brave attempt to recreate a connection that can never be fully salvaged, to work across a distance that is still present, to work across interpretive gaps in language, cosmology, within the interstices of colonial history. At the end of the several weeks of exhibiting the cloak in UCL's North Lodge, Te Urutahi in another FaceTime session, equally as impoverished by a bad cellular connection, gave our cloak a name. We shifted from the North Lodge of UCL to the nearby Geography Department so that we could better hear her tell us that she would now be called *Tukutuku Roimata*, evoking 'The tears of the ancestors from the spiritual realm interwoven and connecting us with the physical realm through the Korowai' (as translated by Kura Puke). These tears recognise the absence of the cloak from a known *whakapapa* as much as they celebrate the emergence of new webs of connection. This name captures both the celebratory qualities of connection brought forth by the communicative possibilities of digital technologies and is also a lament for that which cannot be recovered or reconnected.

A vibrant materiality: experiments in light and sound

Kura and Stuart have been working on the interface of sound and light, converting and translating between the two across space and time, for many years now. During this creation of a virtual *marae* (the ceremonial space in front of and around a meeting house) during the *mihi* (greeting), the voices of Taranaki were translated into colour gel lights that bathed the space, while our voices at UCL were passed through LEDs built into the cloak's case. During the time that the cloak was exhibited at UCL, LED lights built

Figure 46 Hinemihi bathed in light and sound from New Zealand, by Kura Puke and Stuart Foster, June 2014. Reproduced with permission.

into its case transmitted sounds of birdsong and *waiata* from New Zealand, and in the exhibition space we continued to explore an environment in which we moved between different registers of knowledge (genealogy, narratives of making) and different ways of digitising the cloak (converting its image into sound, building 3D images from multiple other images and converting sound into light). This exploration of the materiality of the digital was not simply an aesthetic project, but encouraged us to understand how digitisation works as a technical practice and scaffold for representation. By generating an aesthetic frame for both the content (light and sound) being transmitted and the medium of the transmission (light and sound), this part of the project highlighted the material qualities of the digital interface and in fact intervened into the very idea of the interface or medium.

One of the object lessons provoked by the digitisation of museum objects is a growing awareness of the alternative materiality provided within digital projects. As Kura and Stuart's work with light and sound show, the digital works as a communicative frame not only because of the ways it allows voices from far away to be heard nearby, but also because it shows us things that were always there but that we could never see.[8] It is the presence of technology, rather than its absence, that creates new forms of self-consciousness and new ways of connecting to objects.

The intention of our *mihi* was to activate a Māori space for the cloak, to establish a set of protocols for its care at UCL, and to use digital technologies to create a tangible atmosphere of both light and sound that could relocate the cloak within a Māori environment. Stuart and Kura have left a kit of LED lights and sockets in the Ethnography Collections so that we can now plug the cloak in at any time and channel light and sound from New Zealand directly over her, even as she is in storage. The continued conversion of sound into light and back into sound both drew attention to the material qualities of digital technologies and through their materiality insisted on drawing a parallel between the connectivity of cellular and broadband data flows and the ways in which the Māori cloak also channels flows of *wairua*, or spiritual energy. As Kura insisted, the role of *taonga* is to materialise the energy of recognition and connection. In this way, the digital environment we created worked in two distinct ways – not only did it create new connections, it also instantiated a philosophy of connection that transcended the medium of the digital, encompassed by a Māori cosmology. The digital thus drew attention to its own particular characteristics or affordances, while provoking us to consider how the digital itself may be subsumed by the broader cultural framework of meaning that constitutes aesthetic frames in radically divergent ways.

At the end of the *mihi*, Stuart held the iPad over the cloak to demonstrate how our voices were being translated into the LED lights built into the case. Te Matahiapo in Taranaki were delighted. To show them more, we started to sing, and *waiata* finally rang out in the Octagon Gallery. Kura was happy – despite all of our anxieties, the singing had arrived anyway.

Figure 47 The FaceTime connection between Taranaki and UCL with members of UCL Museums and Anthropology and Ngāti Rānana. Photograph by Pip Guthrie. Reproduced with permission.

The cultural nature of digital objects

I want to highlight how the process of trying to create three-dimensional representations of the cloak pushed our understanding of the creative tensions, limits and materialities of digital technologies – providing an object lesson not just about the nature of our cloak, but also about the digital. The initial question framing the process of creating digital images of the cloak was 'Can you wear a digital cloak?' This question tapped into the current zeitgeist of digitisation projects in museums, which assume that technology can provide engaged experiences equal to, or even better than, the experience of viewing the 'real' object. Given the conservation risks of handling the delicate cloak, we were interested in exploring whether a digital image could in fact be interacted with in a more corporeal way than was permissible with the original artefact. We wanted to explore how digital technologies might facilitate access that transcended the limitations of the cloak's size and fragility and the protective rules of conservation, which ensured that we could display the cloak horizontally only, that we should not touch her with our bare hands or wear her as she was meant to be worn. We started the project with the assumption that the best kind of digital artefact would be a three-dimensional representation of the cloak, so flawlessly photographic that it could be understood to be the most perfect form of simulation, and that we might be able, using avatars and virtual reality, to wear her (visually at least).

In my initial meetings with technologists at UCL, such as those working with the 3D Petrie project (a collaboration between a commercial hardware company working at the cutting edge of 3D scanning and the UCL Egyptology Collections), I began to observe two competing understandings of the process of digitisation that intersect and internalise different aspects of photography.[9] My discussions with 3D specialists demonstrated that digital objects are viewed as repositories of information about the form and structure of objects *and* as visual representations of collections. All too often, the latter was the frame through which the former was accessed. It soon became apparent that a photographically oriented understanding of these digital files dominated museum imaging projects – and that the language used to describe them was fundamentally drawn from the photographic lexicon, even as the process used to construct the images went far beyond that of photography. Following a more expansive position on digital images, gleaned from both anthropology and the interpretive frameworks brought to the project by Kura and our other interlocutors in New Zealand, our digitisation process increasingly moved away from this visual, photographically inclined orientation. It shifted instead towards the capture of alternative haptic states and the incorporation of Māori ways of engaging with objects that were not focused on the visual but understood as images to be located within wider spiritual and social relationships. I articulate this expansive domain as shifting the lexicon of how we understand digital images from terms such as 'index' and 'presence' towards a discourse of co-presence.

Design and engineering technologists working to constitute 3D images of museum collections fundamentally see their work as generating accurate or 'real' representations of the object, aiming for what they term the status of 'digital surrogates'.[10] Digital surrogates not only represent the geometry and measurement of an artefact but also its perceptual qualities. They privilege the visual as the way to generate knowledge about objects. The process of making these digital objects starts photographically, with the construction of point clouds generated by laser scanning, or of large numbers of photographs through the process of photogrammetry, both of which capture data by taking information through light reflected directly from the surface of an object. However, the subsequent processing of this data uses photography as a reference point in terms of texture, colour and so on but departs radically from analogue photographic technologies, using specialist software to create a simulation or model of a photograph (a simulation of indexicality rather than an indexical simulation). These images look like photographs; in fact, it might be argued that they are more photograph-like than many photographs – they seem to be perfect techno-visual light captures of the object. However, the process used to fabricate them is in fact much more akin to that of model-making. The craft of stitching together data and working from photographs to create a digital simulation that effaces the process of its own fabrication is intensively skills-based rather than automatic, and it is it often commented on by software users in museum projects that it is possible to recognise the idiosyncratic hand of the technologist in these perfectly fabricated images.

For instance, Figures 48 and 49 show two digital images: one a screengrab of the three-dimensional rendering of a mummy foot cover in the Petrie collection, the other the regular digital catalogue photograph. The curator of the 3D Petrie project, Margaret Serpico, drew my attention to the simulation of the gold-leaf toes, emphasising her efforts in post-processing to depict a more effective screen simulation of the shining original. As even their reproduction in this book demonstrates, the images present the golden toes in quite different ways.

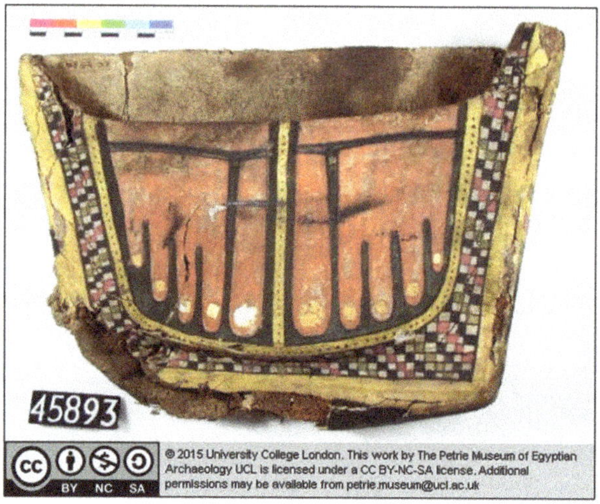

Figure 48, 49 Different web presentations of Egyptian foot cover, UC45893. Top: a digital photograph on the online catalogue petriecat (http://petriecat.museums.ucl.ac.uk/search.aspx); bottom: the same foot cover scanned as part of the 3D Petrie project (http://www.ucl.ac.uk/3dpetriemuseum/3dobjects). © UCL. Reproduced under a CC-BY license.

While a digital surrogate becomes an objective visual fact, software engineers and computer scientists understand it to be, in fact, authored by skilled individuals, and have worked hard to develop protocols and standards for the preservation and documentation of these digital forms.[11] Like the famous natural history dioramas that create a photographic reality effect in three dimensions through the diverse artisanal skills of artists, scientists and taxidermists, 3D digital images should also be understood as models in which creative decisions, grounded in a skilled practitioner knowledge base of understanding materials, enable the production of a new form of second-order mimesis – of photography as well as the original artefact.[12] The 3D digital images are in many instances crafted almost entirely from within a computer to generate visual authority through the production of a photographic aura that evokes rather than denotes direct contact with the object itself.

Despite the success of these images at simulating both the technical process of photography and the museum object, the materiality of the digital image is opaque and ambiguous. Unlike dioramas, or even archival images, which can be recognised as complex artefactual assemblages, and in museum terms are now recognised as genres of material culture in their own right, there is no singular object for a digital image, merely the simulation of one. The three-dimensional likeness that is viewed on the screen gives way to multiple data sets, mediated by several different software platforms and dependent on a varied hardware ecology for its realisation. The act of creating a 3D model is in fact a process of photographic purification, in which photographic metaphors are stripped of their own ambiguities in order to construct what seems like a natural object – the product of a neutral and objective technological process of visualisation. Intensive work goes into producing this kind of photographic effect, stripping away the subjectivity of the curator and programmer, and erasing the perception of a human eye behind the camera and scanner.

I became aware of this complex process partly because of my amateurism and lack of skill in creating these kinds of images. My attempts to use both laser scanning and photogrammetry resulted in images that were lacking in photographic veracity, and the cloak itself seemed to resist capture, as flat surfaces, hair and fibre are notoriously difficult to scan. Our cloak therefore raised many questions regarding the indexicality of data. The dog-hair tassels render the surface difficult to scan using a laser scanner and the form of textiles make them difficult to reconstitute using photogrammetry. Both of these solutions would produce a digital file that *looked just like* the cloak, but was not in fact comprised of information that

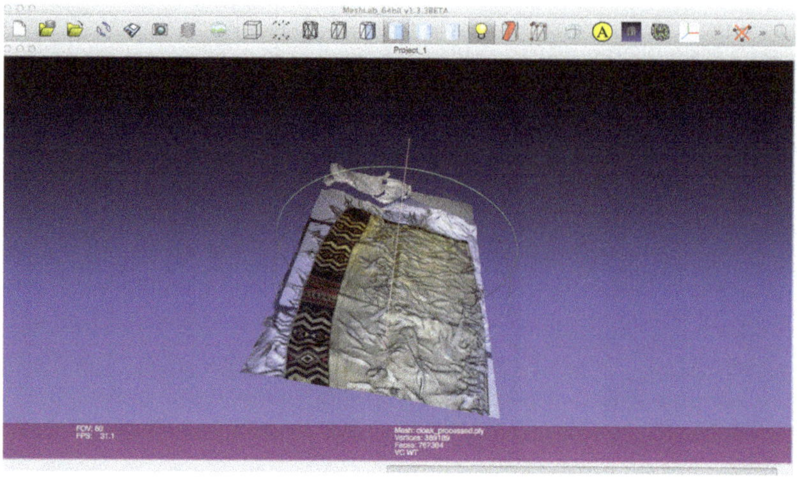

Figure 50 A screengrab of the quick Kinect scan of the cloak.

Figure 51 Screengrab of an attempt to use photogrammetry software to stitch together hundreds of images of the cloak to create a 3D image.

had been taken directly from the cloak (that is, this digital version of the cloak was not a photograph but rather a different kind of visualisation). The cloak challenged our understanding of the process of digitisation in a number of different ways: as a complex artefact that resists the process of digitisation and as a Māori treasure that demands a representational frame that is not fully encapsulated by the ways in which we currently define the predominantly visual experience of photography (which cannot necessarily capture the intangible aspects of an object's character). Indeed, following W.J.T. Mitchell's exhortation to ask 'What do pictures "really" want?', we found a ready series of answers to the question of the cloak's needs, not in the positivism of 3D digitisation as a technology of perfect visual replication, but in a different kind of engagement with digitisation.[13] *Tukutuku Roimata* did not want simply to be seen; it seemed rather that she wanted to return to being active in social networks, fulfilling her destiny as a *taonga* to maintain the connections of *whakapapa*.

Tukutuku Roimata asks us to challenge the process of digitisation in a number of different ways. Just as the virtual *powhiri* was marked by a disjunct between the utopian expectations of digital communication and an imperfect reality, in which gaps of communication and audibility contribute to the ritual, so too does the process of 3D scanning rarely deliver what it is imagined to promise. The cloak was remarkably resistant to all current modes of data capture, providing only sketchy data and demanding a creative engagement to render a visualisation of the object 'as whole'. In order to create a 3D scan that mimetically reproduced the cloak, a different kind of model would have to be crafted. The scanned artefact would provide only partial data. The question is how seriously should we take that imperfect moment – does the partiality of the data capture allow us to learn something about the cloak? Does it highlight the ways in which data may not be a sufficient substitute for information?

Indeed, the very question of creating a digital surrogate is challenged by the nature of textiles that are intended to be seen while worn. The ocular-centric framing of data visualisation that underpins 3D digital object creation diminishes other modes of engagement and what our understanding of a whole object is in terms of both data and its visualisation.

Kura, Stuart and I moved away from visual representations of the cloak, continuing to think about how the process of digitisation fits with the Māori conception of *wairua*, meaning life force or intangible energy. Rather than asking if there can be a digital object (or even trying to create a digital artefact that mimics an object), we thought about the kinds of processes and relationships that are constructed through scanning, photogrammetry and data visualisation. More than just creating an image, the act of displaying relevant digital data has been, for Te Matahiapo, a process of harnessing spiritual energy, and the digital data is rendered as a form of cultural connection and warming, as well as a way of channelling the flows of electrical energy. We worked together to image and experience the cloak as a landscape rather than as an object and used the capacities of digital media to think about a continual oscillation between the visual and the sonic. The networked digital images we worked with in our project engendered a striking experience of co-presence. The *wairua* contained in Māori relationships as they are channelled through *taonga* constitute a profound experience of co-presence in which objects are understood to be experiential links to the past, present and future.

Māori curator and scholar Paul Tapsell has argued that important *taonga*, whether they remain in communities or museums, represent relationships across space and time and between people. He draws on two key metaphors. The first is the delicate tui bird that soars up and around us, weaving up and down between the fabric of space/time for a specific community. Tapsell uses the tui to evoke the sensibility of *taonga* as part of a living community. The second is the comet that reveals itself on special occasions, evoking global awe. Tapsell uses the comet to suggest the ways in which important museum *taonga* continue to resonate for their communities of origin and for others.[14] The framework of *whakapapa* enables Māori people to recognise the interconnections between all beings (animate and inanimate). Important objects and images contain *wairua* and they become energetic channels that continue to produce and reproduce important social relationships.[15] In another digital archive project in New Zealand, Amiria Salmond and her collaborators led by Wayne and Hera Ngata, proposed to substitute the idea of a 'thing' with the Māori term '*mea*', which they used as a top-level category to encompass all other classifications of both the material and the immaterial world, including people, land, sea, objects, houses, projects and ancestors.[16] The emergent theory of the digital is one that sits squarely with broader definitions of culture in this context: a complex articulation of classificatory values that links the material and immaterial, the past and the present.

These Indigenous theories of the generative capacities of digital knowledge structures and processes of translation use Māori understandings of weaving – as a process that is both technological and cosmological – as a way to underpin the cultural understanding of what kinds of digital forms are appropriate for the cloak. Woven objects around the world are used as metaphors of relationality.[17] Māori cloaks are described as objects that warm both the body and the heart. The phrase *to kanoi* means both to weave and to trace ancestry, and cloaks were used traditionally at key life-cycle events including both birth and death.[18] If we consider, as Kura Puke does, digital energy to be a form of warming and a cultural process invested with cultural meaning, rather than a more detached process of visual simulation, we might imagine a very different kind of digital artefact. In fact, if we leave behind the emphasis on the visual in the process of digitisation, and avoid trying to create a simulated environment that by necessity can be apprehended only visually, we might think instead of digital data as cultural information that might be able to connect up to other methods of gathering, storing and presenting information – rather than simply as a tool for a very particular kind of visualisation.

Emergent Māori theories of digital images use the relational and translational qualities of digital media to formulate and represent a worldview: a complex articulation of classificatory values that links the material and immaterial, the past and the present. As a woven *taonga*, *Tukutuku Roimata* sits at the heart of this worldview – not simply as an image of it but as an active participant in its fabrication. In this vein, our imperfect images are not failed visualisations – they became routes for us to understand digital objects as more than just mimetic technologies of visual replication, to see them as experiential domains that can be entered into in order to affect co-presence between people, and between people and things across time and space. Here, Māori expectations mesh with the cutting edge of digital image processing. What happens if we translate the cloak into other kinds of data – for instance, if we merge a digital image of the cloak with a digital version of a Māori weaving chant? Or if we translate a digitised chant or song into a visual image? We are now experimenting with converting the digital images into sound files to be heard in an immersive environment and we are also using gaming software to convert the scanned data into topographical representations that the viewer can fly over and through. This perspective meshes much better with a nascent Māori museology, developed by curators such as Paul Tapsell, Huhana Smith and Arapata Hakiwai, in which objects and people are linked through *whakapapa*, grounded fundamentally through links to Indigenous landscapes.[19]

Te Ara Wairua has therefore been more than just a celebratory demonstration of the ways in which digital technologies can fulfil their utopian promise to bring greater connectivity, accessibility and visibility to collections. Rather, the project explored how the process of digitisation may be located within different cultural frameworks, producing very different expectations of digital objects from the ones that we started within

Figure 52 Still from a rendering of the cloak as a landscape using gaming software.

the museum. Instead of pushing for a heightened indexicality, or simulation, of the original object, our digital activities extended *Tukutuku Roimata*, allowing her to fulfil her potential as a *taonga* to connect across time and space. Our communicative network was filled with *wairua*, with chant and with song. These experiments, some of which seemed to have 'failed', have provided in object lesson in unpacking the cultural determinisms of digital media, exposing its flexibility, multiplicity and multisensory affordances.

Mimesis, replication and reality

I started this book with what might be perceived as the most analogue of objects: a wooden box, handmade to contain glass lantern-slides. I ended with a digital rendering of a cloak as a landscape, moving beyond conventional museum imaging techniques that simulate the look of an object to evoke a Māori way of valuing treasured cultural possessions. But working from the first to the last, it seems clear that all of these object lessons demonstrate that there is no clear division between the digital and the analogue. All of the projects described here show a marked continuum between different museum technologies. By bringing together objects such as the Web version of the Malakulan rambaramp and a pen with which the decorative arts are collected, these objects demonstrate that both knowledge and sociality in museums are

Figure 53 Screengrab from *Bears on Stairs*. This computer-designed animation was printed in 3D and the objects were then filmed using stop-motion animation. Source: https://vimeo.com/91711011. Reproduced under fair use.

established by a range of different technologies, which are always culturally inflected and constituted. The digital is but the latest in a string of interpretive and imaging technologies devised to copy, distribute and presence collections. As the still from the animation *Bears on Stairs* demonstrates, digital technologies are deeply entangled in the contemporary production of material culture.[1] Parry's notion of the 'post-digital' museum recognises that the digital has become such an integral part of everyday museum practice that the separation of digital departments from other divisions in museums is fast becoming historical.[2] Rather, digital skills and practices are entangled in all museum operations – from collecting through to exhibition design and display. This entanglement also needs to extend to the ways in which we appreciate the very nature of museum collections.

In her book, *Material Participation*, Noortje Marres argues for a new way of understanding the interaction between people and digital technologies (among other material forms). She argues that the language of agency reifies a very particular division between the material and the social, the subjective and the objective. Marres suggests that the framework of material participation presents a more hybrid understanding of the entanglement of technology with social action and public engagement. She explores 'device-centred' perspectives on participation that distinguish a 'performative politics of things'.[3] This performative politics is very much on display in digital museum projects, which project utopian ideals about technology as much as they do collections.

I have been working with a number of concepts that allow us to bridge the divide between digital and analogue. The idea of the 'contact zone', like Marres' notion of participation, allows us to theorise objects not just in terms of their material qualities but in terms of the social relations and political hierarchies that structure engagement with them. The concept, and process, of design is also often used to explain the ways in which material forms are brought together in particular patterns, which are deeply implicated in the politics of mass production and consumption. Notions of materials, materiality and material culture have some core principles in common that help us to understand the entwined material and conceptual foundations of digital objects. As a body of social theory, these paradigms insist on the mutual constitution between subject and object, person and thing; they challenge any clear-cut border between the cultural and natural world; and they celebrate the vibrant efficacy of form.

As well as arguing for a kind of dissolution of the digital into a broader material world, I am also interested in what objects such as the pen can teach us about the nature of digital objects, and the ways in which the digital form is increasingly built into our definition of the museum collection. The pen itself, as a digital–analogue hybrid, was developed as an interface between the collections, the visitor and the museum database. This interface demonstrates the ways in which the translation of knowledge about collections across and between media has been radically naturalised. This translation is by no means effected only through the digital but has a much longer trajectory within museums in which different representational media have long mimetically worked to destabilise the boundary between representation and reality. As my account of our quest to image the Māori cloak, *Tukutuku Roimata*, in the UCL Ethnography Collections shows, photography in particular has been exploited for its apparent indexicality as a tool of mimetic translation in museums.

The social spaces of exhibition halls and their resolute multidimensionality complicate many of our representational theories that take photography as a template. Consider, for instance, one of the famed diorama in the American Museum of Natural History, this one part of the African People's Hall, curated by Colin Turnbull in the 1960s. It presents a tableau of nomads in the Atlas Mountains at dawn. The caption for the diorama references the exact time of day, the moment of sunrise: '*The Saghru looking north to the Atlas Mountains, Morocco. The sky is as it would have been seen from here on July 18, 1932, at 4am.*'

Figure 54 Berber diorama, Hall of African Peoples, American Museum of Natural History. Photograph by D. Finnin ©AMNH/D. Finnin. Reproduced with permission.

The diorama indexes a specific moment of time – it may very well have been copied from a photograph. It is helpful to think about the capacities of museum displays to mimetically reproduce indexicality, working much like photographs to presence the real. As Jonathan Crary has noted for public spectacles in the nineteenth century, the experience of spectacle was recognised as predominantly visual.[4] The emphasis on *visual* culture has not only blinded us to the full range of the corporeal sensorium, it has developed an understanding of representation that draws primarily on a two-dimension visual image as a template (of which the photograph may be seen as the perfect example).[5] Michael Taussig's discussion of mimesis, as 'the nature that culture uses to create second nature, the faculty to copy, imitate, make models, explore difference, yield into and become Other', might be a better way in which to understand the interfaces I have been discussing here, whereby digital technologies remediate, remix, translate and substitute for older collections, in the process creating new perceptions of the real, new relationships to artefacts, and to the past.[6]

The photographic veracity of museum dioramas is obscured in the present day by our heightened perception of their materiality. It is by now widely acknowledge that displays such as the dioramas at the AMNH were produced by skilled artists, and museum preparators today still delight in inserting small marks of their own craft into the displays at the museum.[7] As we saw in the case of the Māori cloak at UCL, popular understandings of digital imaging of collections still largely ignore the hand of the technician. Digital images, from 3D screen images to 3D printed scans, are largely perceived to mechanically index the original. This is strange because the materials and media used in techniques such as 3D printing are still generally unlike that of the original and considerable work has to go into both their production and the sense of replication experienced by their viewers. The medium of 3D printing is almost willed away through an interpretive sleight of hand that focuses on the magic of conjuring a solid artefact out of a supposedly immaterial image. This sense of magic will be familiar to many of us who have read Roald Dahl's book, *Charlie and the Chocolate Factory*. One of Willy Wonka's most intriguing inventions is a giant chocolate bar that is shrunk in the factory, then teleported into the airwaves to be plucked by the viewer from the screen of their television. This sense of wondrous replacement through replication could be said to be mirrored in the ways in which we perceive 3D-printed museum collections.[8]

Figure 55 3D print of the Arch of Den, Palmyra, installed in Trafalgar Square, London, 20 April 2016. Photograph by Manateedugong. Reproduced under a CC BY-NC-ND 2.0 license. Source: https://flic.kr/p/Gu7Hqa.

In April 2016, the Institute of Digital Archaeology, a joint project of Oxford and Harvard universities, printed a 3D replica of the Triumphal Arch of the Temple of Bel in Palmyra, Syria, that had just been destroyed by ISIS militants, and erected it in London's Trafalgar Square. Boris Johnson, London's mayor at that time, heralded the newly printed arch as a 'two fingers to Daesh' gesture, and the arch has now also been displayed in New York.[9] The media paid little attention to the materiality or formal and aesthetic qualities of the reproduction, focusing on the redemptive power of digital imaging to reproduce lost heritage, a form of salvage not dissimilar to the original urges to collect the material culture of the 'disappearing worlds' of colonised peoples in the nineteenth century. The Institute, working with UNESCO, has also distributed hundreds of 3D cameras to local volunteers, asking them to document as much as possible of Syria's archaeological heritage. The *Million Images Project* aims to create a crowd-sourced databank of images that can be used in virtual reconstruction projects. The *Million Images Project* allows the visitor, wearing 3D glasses, to see images of vulnerable heritage, much of which may no longer be there. Similarly, 3D experiences of sensitive sites such as the caves at Lascaux or the pyramids of Giza, much like the *Google*

Art Project, are presented as political mediators, ways to side-step unsavoury political regimes and the challenges of the entwined processes of environmental and social degradation.

Like the *Google Art Project*'s vision of Holbein's *The Ambassadors*, these new digital forms contain a politics that re-presents these objects in a digital space, proscribing our way of seeing and experiencing, and overwriting this politics through a fantastical and sensuously overloaded form of mimesis, which Taussig might define as a form of 'mimetic excess'. Yet it is also our responsibility to ask: what kinds of objects emerge as the existing collections are mimetically replaced in such different materials and milieus? What vision of the real world do they produce and what do we do with it?

A recent exhibition at the Venice Biennale, curated by the Victoria and Albert Museum, *A World of Fragile Parts* (2016), presented different efforts to reproduce collections, including a 3D print of an illicit scan by the artists Nora Al-Badri and Jan Nikolai Nelles of the bust of Nefertiti held at the Neues Museum in Berlin.[10] This is the final object lesson of my book and is also pictured on its cover. In December 2015, the two artists released 3D scanned data into the public domain along with a video showing how they had clandestinely stolen the data during museum visits by walking around the bust with Kinect scanners hidden under their coats.[11] Alongside the open source provision of data and the video, the project has also included a true-to-original 3D print of the bust and a discussion hosted by the artists in Cairo of the relationship between contemporary art and heritage.[12] The artists called their project *The Other Nefertiti* and used the hack to propose both a virtual repatriation of Nefertiti, allowing a printed version of the bust to be made visible in Egypt for the first time since her removal, as well as drawing an analogy between the subversive way in which the data was collected and the original collection of the object, which has long been seen by the Egyptian government as emerging from illegal tomb-raiding, and illicit archaeology in Egypt by European archaeologists.[13] This, however, was not the end of the story. In the wake of *Nefertiti 2.0,* a series of enquiries raised by technologists and journalists raised the question of whether or not it would have been possible for the handheld scanners used by Al-Badri and Nelles to have captured the data released by the artists. Journalists traced a probable source of the data to a much higher-resolution scan commissioned by the Neues Museum itself, made by a private company, which has not been made available to the public. The website of this company presents a scan of Nefertiti that is uncannily like the image released by Al-Badri and Nelles. The artists responded by claiming that they had no specialist technical knowledge and were using data and resources managed by hackers whom they refused to name. If the sceptics are right, then the project is in fact a double hack: drawing attention to museum hoarding not just of ancient collections but of their digital doubles and using the tools of data collection and presentation to undo the regimes of authority and property over which the museum still asserts sovereignty, mocking the redemptive claims of so-called 'digital repatriation'.[14]

Questions of authenticity of the data, of museum sovereignty, of distribution and access have been extended into the digital domain – even within the journalistic obsession with the 'real' origins of the data co-opted by Nelles and Al-Badri for their project. I propose that we follow Taussig and understand these technical interventions as a form of 'sympathetic magic for the postcolonial age', a way of capturing the real as a form not of simple replication but rather as a kind of mimetic excess in which the technical practices of mimesis constitute not just a version of objectivity but a form of politics itself.[15] As a form of mimesis, *Nefertiti 2.0* draws our attention to the work that the digital does to construct media

Figure 56 *The Other Nefertiti*. 2017. 3D print and digital file. © Nora Al- Badri and Jan Nikolai Nelles. Reproduced with permission.

ideologies, both in reifying existing conceptual and material orders and provoking a radical re-examination of their future.

All of the object lessons I have presented here contain an implicit provocation about circulation and return. As objects are transformed from one medium into another, what opportunities, and challenges, does this process of mediation raise for conventional museum discourses of ownership and to the politics of deciding where collections should be? Why, within the context of the largely celebratory discourses of digital technologies, are museums still reluctant to let go of their collections and, in some instances, their data? The proliferation of new digital objects of circulation provokes an anxiety in both museums and communities that contradicts many of the utopian discourses of openness that characterise the age of Web 2.0.[16]

The mimetic faculty of digital renderings (visual or otherwise) has shifted the weight of intellectual authority away from collections into their digital counterparts. Yet, as all of the projects here have shown, the digital is dependent on existing and multiple forms of collections. It is better to think about the interface between different material forms, and between objects and people, than it is to think about either the digital or the analogue in isolation from one another.[17]

This last point could take us to a central argument that has been salient throughout these different object lessons – to posit that *the digital does not exist*. There is no essential quality of the digital that links all of these projects. Rather, by observing the digital as another kind of thing in the world, we may begin to understand how the digital encompasses a plethora of different representational forms, techniques and technologies that work in different ways to develop different kinds of object lessons. By asserting that the digital does not exist, we must not however assume that there is no such thing as a digital object. The politics of 'material participation' that the digital effects in our understanding of the real world as a set of refractions from one kind of object to another are yet to be fully uncovered. As I have explored here, the digital is a complex artefact that, like any other, renders knowledge and information material in ways that have profound effects, emphasising 'a digital terrain that is enmeshed with the everyday practical and often-times messy and contradictory fields of relation, respect, and reciprocity that cannot be reduced to a singular metaphor'.[18]

Ending here with the contentious statement that the digital does not exist is of course a provocation. I do not intend to negate all of the complex thinking, collaborative work, material infrastructures and financial investments that have been put into digital museum projects. Rather,

I have been questioning how our assumptions about how the material, social and political foundations of digital media establish an important object lesson for the start of the twenty-first century. We – museum visitors, curators, scholars, artists, activists, members of the public, members of counter-publics and citizens – as both producers and consumers of digital content, are also the custodians of digital culture. We have a responsibility to engage in the infrastructures of law, ethics, care and attention that structure our digital lives. We play a part in generating the knowledge fields and informational networks that constitute a large part of digital collections. Only by understanding where these objects come from can we influence where they will go in the future.

Notes

Introduction

1. 'Object Lesson.' Definition taken from Merriam-Webster.com. Merriam-Webster, n.d. Web. http://www.merriam-webster.com/dictionary/object lesson (last accessed 6 October 2017).
2. Daston (2007: 16).
3. The global museum boom has been described from a number of different perspectives. For a select bibliography: Boylan (2006) gives an overview of the global expansion of the museum profession; Williams (2007) discusses the global emergence of memorial museums; Werner (2005) and Bishop (2014) discuss the expansion of the global contemporary art museum; Wang and Rowlands (2017) discuss the museum boom in China; and Stanley (1998), Hendry (2005), Webster (1990) and Issac (2007) discuss the global emergence of cultural centres and identity-focused museums.
4. See Kelty *et al.* (2015) for a discussion of the ways in which political ideologies and epistemological framings of participation are produced within internet and new media projects, and Graham (2016) for a discussion of the techniques by which co-production is maintained in museums.
5. Barbara Kirschenblatt Gimblett talks about the 'surgical' process of making meaning and context through the display of objects in her influential article, 'Objects of Ethnography' (1991).
6. This image persists, notwithstanding the fact that most digital media in museums may suffer more from wear and tear than other displays. The first museum fieldwork I ever undertook was for my undergraduate final-year dissertation when I worked for a summer at the Natural History Museum in London evaluating visitor interactions with their multimedia displays. As well as leaving the galleries every day with a splitting headache, my ethnography observed how the desire of many people to push buttons indiscriminately often ran counter to the design of interactive displays, which would frequently break, leading one museum employee to describe the digital components of the display as more 'hyperactive than interactive'. Griffiths (2008: 274–82) has a similar critique of the way in which discourses of interactivity have been deployed in relation to 'new media' in museums.
7. Bakke (2016) and Starosielski (2015) discuss the material foundations of the electricity and telecommunications infrastructures that underpin the World Wide Web. Hu presents a pre-history of the cloud, exploring how our vision of the immaterial information web is prefigured within older material and imaginary networks, arguing that we need to stand at a 'middle distance … not wholly immersed in either its virtuality or its materiality' (2015: XX).
8. Jonathan Sterne has developed the frame of Format Theory within his important account of the development of the MP3 format (2012). Platform Studies aims to excavate the structures of digital media, in both hardware and software; see, for example, Manovich (2013), Kirschenbaum (2012) and the Platform Studies Series published by MIT Press.
9. Daston (2007: 20), see also Henning (2007).
10. Thinking of the digital as material continues a well-established analytic trajectory; see Shep (2016), Leonardi (2010), Blanchette (2011), Pink *et al.* (2016).

11. See for example, a recent book by Steven Conn (2010) in which he asks '*Do Museums Still Need Objects?*' Conn surveys contemporary debates about repatriation, the connections between education and entertainment, and challenges the relevance and legacy of the implicitly nineteenth-century collection for the museum as a site of civic engagement.
12. Clifford writes, drawing from Pratt (1991): 'When museums are seen as contact zones, their organizing structure as a *collection* becomes an ongoing historical, political, moral *relationship* – a power-charged set of exchanges, or push and pull. The organizing structure of the museum-as-collection functions like Pratt's frontier. A center and a periphery are assumed: the center a point of gathering, the periphery an area of discovery ... A contact perspective views all culture-collecting strategies as responses to particular histories of dominance, hierarchy, resistance, and mobilization. And it helps us see how claims to both universalism and to specificity are related to concrete social locations' (1997: 192–3, 213, emphasis in original).
13. Manovich (2013).
14. See, for example, Vergo (1989), Hooper-Greenhill (1992), Bennett (1995), Henare (2005a).
15. As Fiona Candlin argues through her study of 'micromuseums' – museums that sit far from capital cities, curated by local enthusiasts, sometimes even obsessives – we need to unmoor museum studies from being defined only by canonical, discipline-based, national museums, exhibitions that are visited by hundreds of thousands of people. Candlin asks how looking at smaller, less famous museums might enable 'researchers to reconceive notions of curation, collections, the public, and what it means to visit a museum' Candlin (2015: 2).
16. Here I join with a number of historians and media theorists who explore the historical trajectories of 'new' media as they continue to return in different forms. See Gitelman (2006), Gitelman and Pingree (2004) and Griffiths (2008).

Chapter 1

1. This history is comprehensively presented and theorised in Bennett (1995), Findlen (1996), Conn (1998), Stocking (1985), Hooper-Greenhill (1992).
2. See for example, O'Hanlon and Welsch (2000), Clifford (1988), Alberti and Hallam (2013). Gosden *et al.* (2007) reframe the Pitt Rivers Museum in Oxford as a 'relational museum' composed of networks of friendship, patronage and scholarship spreading both across the world and across the nineteenth and twentieth centuries.
3. Were and King (2012) explore a number of idiosyncratic case studies that retell the normative history of museums from the vantage point of its margins. Candlin (2015) describes an alternative genealogy of smaller, often private, museums in her book, *Micromuseology*.
4. One of the most famous perhaps of these is P.T. Barnum's famous American Museum, which burned to the ground in downtown New York in 1895 (see Harris 1981, Irmscher 1999). The museum has been recreated as an immersive digital experience: http://lostmuseum.cuny.edu (last accessed 15 August 2016).
5. The Museum of Jurassic Technology in Los Angeles is dedicated to a number of idiosyncratic exhibits that confound and draw our attention to assumptions about truth, reality and indexicality in museum technologies of display and exhibition. Past exhibitions include Dogs of the Soviet Space Program, the Microminiatures of Hagop Sandaldjian, and the Stink Ant of Cameroon, all of which challenge our sense of reality, leading us to question the limits of museums as rational sites of learning. See Weschler (1997) for a long discussion of the museum.
6. Greenblatt (1991: 42).
7. Haraway's discussion (1984) of the broader political and gender relations underpinning the production of the Hall of African Mammals is a foundational example of this. Bennet *et al.* (2017) discuss the parallel histories of museums in North America, France, Indochina, the UK, Australia and New Zealand and highlight the ways in which museums became instruments of 'collecting, ordering, and governing'.
8. See Briggs (1988) for a broader articulation of the resonance of 'Victorian Things'. Stocking (1985) and Jenkins (1994) have extensively discussed the object lessons of nineteenth-century ethnographic museums. Edward Said's famous articulation of Orientalism (2003[1978]) also focuses on the nineteenth century as pivotal in the consolidation of the Western view of the Oriental other, and Barringer and Flynn (1998) expand Said's perspective to look at the

colonial underpinnings of nineteenth-century museum projects. Coombes (1997) explores the entanglement of colonial and national identity formation in the project of collecting in Africa.

9. Writers such as Cuno (2008, 2009), Appiah (2006) and Brown (2003) survey the contested terrain of cultural property and ownership of collections. All of these authors celebrate the capacity of the museum to own and represent other people's heritage. Indigenous curators and authors such as Amy Lonetree (2012) and Nancy Mithlo (2004), alongside artists such as Fred Wilson (see Corrin, 1994), Andrea Fraser (2007), Jolene Rickard (2007) and Paul Chaat Smith (2009), are far more critical of museums, calling for their decolonisation and the denaturalisation of their claims to be the proper place for cultural heritage and cultural property.
10. Tylor (1881: 458).
11. For a thorough overview of the making and resonance of the Pitt Rivers Museum, see Gosden *et al.* (2007) and O'Hanlon (2014).
12. Much of this work focuses on reconnecting the nineteenth-century collections to source communities and working within a globally expansive, collaborative register. See Alison Brown and Laura Peers' work with Blackfoot communities (2013) and Krmpotich and Peers' work with Haida (2013). This museological perspective is explored beyond the Pitt Rivers in the edited volume *Museums and Source Communities* (Peers and Brown, 2003).
13. Fenton (1984: 38). The scholars working in the Pitt Rivers have also generated some seminal research into the poetics of the museum and archive; for instance, Elizabeth Edwards' work on anthropological photography and archives, *Raw Histories* (2001), and the edited collection *Sensible Objects*, which explores the sensory registers of colonial collections (Edwards *et al.*, 2006).
14. Haraway's seminal account of the creation of the Natural History dioramas (1984) needs to be linked to accounts of the museum and its continued poetics in contemporary New York (e.g. Jacknis 2002, 2004). Glass (2009) and Jacknis (1985) focus specifically on Boas and the production of life groups. Boas himself commented on the tensions within life group displays in a series of intense discussions about museum technologies that led to his resignation from the museum (e.g. Boas 1907).
15. See Hinsley and Wilcox (2016).
16. Griffiths (2002, 2008) see also Crary (1999).
17. See Glass (2011) for a sensitive re-evaluation of this historical period of collecting and a proposal for a new museological framing for these collections.
18. See Parkin (2009).
19. Tony Bennett has referred to the 'Exhibitionary Complex' to signal the ways in which seeing, and looking, were drawn into forms of governmentality (1988).
20. See Edwards *et al.* (2006), Kenderdine (2016).
21. See Vergo (1989), Hooper-Greenhill (1994) and Hein (2000).
22. As argued by Sherry Turkle in her book *Alone Together* (2012).
23. As discussed by Shirky (2009), Kelty (2008), Gerbaudo (2012), Coleman (2012), Morozov (2012).
24. Lev Manovich (2013) surveys the software through which most of our digital experiences are mediated. Gabrys (2011) unravels the material infrastructures that support the production and destruction of digital material culture, and Starosielski (2015) describes the invisible infrastructures and networks that facilitate the World Wide Web.
25. As described by Tony Bennett in *The Birth of the Museum* (1995).
26. I survey these debates and positions in Geismar (2012).
27. These projects are surveyed at http://www.metmuseum.org/blogs/digital-underground (last accessed 28 September 2017).

Chapter 2

1. Boas (1907); see also Jacknis (1985).
2. Boas (1907: 924); see also Boas (1897).
3. See Isaac (2008) for the context and wider discussion around this image.
4. At the pinnacle of Heye's collecting there was a joke in Indian country that all he left behind after visiting an Indian village was a naked Indian holding a fistful of cash. This anecdote is ruefully described by Gerald Vizenor (2011: 144), who also contributed the concept of 'survivance' to the underlying museological principles of the National Museum of the American

Indian, curated with the insistence that American Indians from both hemispheres have survived the incursions of colonialism, collecting and representational hegemony. The notion of profusion at NMAI may also therefore be read this way, as an insistence on each object being recognised as an index of a native person or peoples not just in the terms of anthropological theory but within Indigenous epistemologies.

5. See Boellstorff (2016) and Nardi (2015) for a rehearsal of many of these debates around virtuality.
6. For a good discussion of the expansive interpretive and philosophical frames that inflect material culture studies, see Miller (1987), Miller and Tilley (1996) and Hicks (2010).
7. Glass (2009); see also Hinsley and Holm (1976).
8. Stocking (1985).
9. Griffiths (2008). David Jenkins argues that the systematic collection and arrangement of objects in the nineteenth century gave rise to a metonymic interpretive frame in which 'object, context, and text-metonymic substitution, objectification, and classification characterized museum exhibits and provided the basis for the authority of visual displays' (1994: 268).
10. Bennett (1995).
11. Clifford (1997).
12. Mithlo (2004), Boast (2011).
13. Rosanna Raymond is an accomplished artist and researcher who has written extensively on the politics of reconnecting with historic links and has explored this both in text and artistic practice. See Raymond and Salmond (2008), Raymond (2003).
14. The digital is such a vast category that it is worth thinking about the differences between digital media – the ways in which the digital has become a representational domain – and digital technologies – the ways in which the digital provides the form for many different kinds of practices and operations (see Geismar, 2013a).
15. For some utopianist perspectives, see Shirky (2009) and Costa *et al.* (2016). For some dystopian perspectives, see Turkle (2012) and Morozov (2012).
16. Hui (2012: 387).
17. Pink *et al.* (2016: 10). This perspective on the digital as a process rather than a thing is also taken by Kallinikos *et al.*, in which they explore how digital objects are characterised by the qualities, or affordances, of editability, interactivity, openness and distributedness (2010; see also Kallinokos *et al.*, 2013).
18. Manovich (2013).
19. Horst and Miller define the digital as 'all that which can be ultimately reduced to binary code but which produces a further proliferation of particularity and difference' (2012: 3). As scholars such as Evens have commented, 'materiality is indispensable, it haunts the digital, but the digital's distinction, its particular way of being, derives from its erosion of materiality, its embrace of the abstract'. (2012: 14).
20. Larkin (2013) reviews contemporary theories of infrastructure, drawing on this key definition. See also Star's seminal article on the ethnography of infrastructure (1999). A recent section of *Cultural Anthropology*'s 'Theorizing the Contemporary' focuses on 'Evil Infrastructures', with a disproportionate amount of contributions focusing on the digital and the ways in which platforms, data and networks can be used counter to the utopian vision of connectivity, accessibility and openness (see https://culanth.org/fieldsights/1117-evil-infrastructures, last accessed 15 August 2017).
21. This is even though recent work on digital piracy emphasises the effects of reproduction on the affectivity of the digital image, creating grainy, pixelated and corrupted image worlds, e.g. Steyerl (2009).
22. See Horst and Miller (2012), introduction to the first edition of the volume *Digital Anthropology*, which highlights the ways in which digital technologies are imbricated in both socio-cultural worlds and within social theory. See also Hjorth *et al.* (2017) for a survey of contemporary applications and insights from the field of digital ethnography, which highlights the intersections of digital media and social research methods. Manuel Castells has theorised our current time as that of the 'Network Society' (2000), which has generated new forms of participation such as crowdsourcing (Shirky, 2009), flashmobs (Rheingold, 2003), citizen journalism and participatory media (Fish, 2017), hacking (Coleman, 2012) and open source (Kelty, 2008); see also Barney *et al.* (2016).
23. Kelty (2008) describes this entanglement of materiality and sociality in software as 'recursive', calling, for example, open source software a 'recursive public'.

24. These examples are described in Kelty (2008), Gell (1998) and Miller (2010) respectively.
25. See, for instance, a recent article by Harding and Martin (2016) in which they discover the hall for the first time in 2016, and understand it as an unchanged anachronism without appreciating its complex history and the interesting transformations that have been effected within it over the course of the twentieth century. They also argue strongly for the hall to be updated. See also Jacknis (2004, 2015).
26. These initiatives include the influential exhibition *From Totems To Turquoise* (Chalker *et al.*, 2004), a collaboration with tribes of the Grande Ronde Community of Oregon to sign the Willemette Meteorite Agreement, with an accompanying museum internship for tribal youth, as well as many collaborative research projects.
27. http://www.amnh.org/exhibitions/permanent-exhibitions/human-origins-and-cultural-halls/hall-of-northwest-coast-indians/digital-totem (last accessed 16 August 2017).
28. Celebrated in the media (e.g. Carvajal, 2017). Not everyone in the Northwest Coast is comfortable with being on display in the museum in such a way (anonymous curator, personal communication, August 2017).
29. http://www.amnh.org/explore/ology/at-the-museum/dreams-of-the-haida-child (last accessed 31 October 2017).
30. Press Release, 'American Museum of Natural History Begins Major Project to Restore and Update Historic Northwest Coast hall', 25 September 2017.
31. Manovich (2013: 15).
32. Kallinikos *et al.* (2013: 357). Knox and Walford (2016) ask if there is such thing as a digital ontology. They comment: 'In drawing attention to the ontological dimensions of digital technologies, we want to explore what happens when we attend to the affordances, agencies, and logics of digital devices themselves, as they participate in making social worlds... One benefit of this ontological approach is that it allows us to pay attention to the unexpected or unforeseen effects of digital technologies and their capacity to disrupt, destabilize, rechannel, unsettle, all the while calling forth different ways of relating.'
33. Kallinikos *et al.* (2010, 2013).
34. Geismar (2013a).
35. Deger (2006, 2008, 2016) has a sustained project tracking Aboriginal media production in Australia as a distinctively Indigenous form and aesthetic.
36. Were (2014: 135).
37. Küchler (1997).
38. Brown (2007), and see the chapter on Cloak within this book.
39. Ngata *et al.* (2012: 242).
40. See for instance Geismar and Mohns (2011).
41. Povinelli (2011), Christen (2005).
42. See, for instance, Christie and Verran (2013), Glass (2015), Hogsden and Poulter (2012) and Salmond (2013).
43. Rowley (2013), Phillips (2011).
44. http://mukurtu.org, see Christen (2011, 2012). A demonstration of the knowledge protocols that Christen developed into Mukurtu can be found here: http://vectorsjournal.org/projects/index.php?project=67 (last accessed 20 August 2017).
45. Anderson and Christen (2013) and Anderson (2012).
46. www.localcontexts.org (last accessed 31 October 2017).
47. Aboriginal Australian remix is described by Christen (2005) and by Deger (2016).
48. Such projects align with digital movements such as WikiLeaks, and digital practices such as remix (see Christen, 2005). They also raise the issue of the 'Faustian contract' that Faye Ginsburg (1991) has eloquently raised in exploring Indigenous film and video projects, and reflect tensions in the museum contact zone that Mithlo describes as the 'red man's burden' (2004). Both Mithlo and Ginsburg sensitively evaluate the role that Indigenous peoples play in institutional settings, recognising that new media does not necessarily necessitate new forms of social and political relations (see also Ginsburg, 2008).
49. Hollinger *et al.* (2013).
50. The communities at Zuni Pueblo, for example, are highly critical of the notion of digital repatriation (see Boast and Enote, 2013); see also Isaac (2015) on several imaging projects run by the Smithsonian and their philosophical and cultural after-effects.

Chapter 3

1. Dudley (2012: 5).
2. This was largely due to the influence of structural theory, and subsequently post-structuralism, which considered language, especially written language, as the ultimate representational form and used text as a reference point for understanding the process of representation and meaning.
3. I use the term 'material culture studies' broadly and non-canonically to include pretty much all branches of what has also been referred to as 'the material turn'. A foundational text for the renewed theoretical interest in anthropology and archaeology is Daniel Miller's *Material Culture and Mass Consumption* (1987), which draws on Hegel, Simmel and Munn to develop a position on the mutual constitution of people and things as a Hegelian process of subjectification and objectification. Arjun Appadurai's edited volume *The Social Life of Things* (1988) continues to influence scholarship on objects with a methodological and conceptual tracking of commodities across time and space in order to understand their value. Bruno Latour's work in actor–network theory, and most especially on the condition of modernity, has also been influential in breaking down interpretive divides between people and things (1993). Within anthropology and in relation to ethnographic objects, the edited volume *Thinking Through Things* (Henare, 2007) asserts a perspective on material culture that does not separate objects and language, but argues for the object as a vital interpretive site, drawing on the philosophy of Wittgenstein, the work of science and technology studies and actor–network theory, and the anthropology of Marilyn Strathern, Roy Wagner and Eduardo Viveiros de Castro (see Geismar 2011 for a summary of some of these debates). Other influential publications, which exemplify only a small portion of a large and growing field, include Alfred Gell's posthumous book *Art and Agency* (1998), which argues for a perspective on art as agentive and socially efficacious rather than simply representational; Jane Bennett's *Vibrant Matter* (2010), which argues for 'a political ecology of things', bringing material culture studies into political science; Caroline Bynum's *Christian Materiality* (2015), which exemplifies the ways in which these arguments have been picked up in art history; Bill Brown's *Thing Theory* (2001) and Jonathan Lamb's work on object narratives, *The Things Things Say* (2011), which demonstrates the resonance of this approach within literary theory. This list is by no means comprehensive but rather signals the widespread attention to objects within academic thinking.
4. See MacGregor (2012), Geismar (2008).
5. See Wilkes (2011), Howes and Laughlin (2012) and Miodownik (2015) on the conceptual work of materials libraries.
6. I draw these quotes from Ingold (2007: 14). This nature-focused perspective on materials is echoed in Jane Bennett's book *Vibrant Matter* (2010), which draws on the work of Donna Haraway and Bruno Latour and is situated within the framework of 'New Materialism' (Connolly, 2013, Coole and Frost, 2010). Rather than a romantic understanding of nature as something a priori to be tamed and civilised by culture, or a (post-)structuralist understanding of nature as a set of symbols meaningfully brought into being through culture or as a system of meaning that can be put together, and taken apart, Bennett's notion of vibrancy presents us with a view of a world of shimmering substance, and posits an ineluctable and insistent framework of form as the starting place for interpretive work. Similarly, Ingold uses a notion of materials to bypass social, historical and political context, and focus on more general understandings of embodied experience. These approaches are often described as post-humanist, attempting to bypass the domination of human beings and their culture in the production of meaningful lived experiences. As I explain below, I am sceptical of this displacement and agree with Severin Fowles (2016), who argues that this further subjugates the object to human analysis, creating a 'perfect subject' that cannot speak back to the analyst.
7. See Ingold (2007, 2013), Harvey *et al.* (2013).
8. Ingold (2007).
9. Miodownik (2013).
10. Mintz (1986), Tsing (2015), Barry (2013), Harvey and Knox (2015), Drazin and Küchler (2015).
11. Drazin (2015: xvii). This perspective moves away from the post-humanist theorisation of materials, drawing more explicitly on the French anthropology of technology that has explored the ways in which technological practices and processes link people and materials within a telos of production and making; e.g. Mauss (2006), Coupaye (2013), Lemonnier (2012).

12. Unpublished AHRC Ethnographic Documentation Project Report, UCL 2008.
13. See Russell (1987) and Hill (2006).
14. 'There was a series of dispersals of "unwanted ethnographic material" from the Willesden store, which was vacated after the Second World War. The material was temporarily transferred to the British Museum, which was first allowed to choose any material for its collections, through its representative H.J. Braunholz, who also advised on the dispersal in general. A quantity of material was also sent to the Liverpool Museum, which had lost much of its collection due to bomb damage during the war. The rest of the material was disposed of in what have become known as the "ten distributions", which took place between 1919 and 1954. On each occasion a circular letter was sent out to the curators of selected British museums inviting them to attend on a particular day to select items for their collections. The material left at the end of each distribution, known as the "residue", was often sold to a dealer, K.A. Webster. At the end of all ten distributions, however, there was still a very large quantity of material left and much of this was offered to institutions abroad.' (source: www.wellcomelibrary.org, section on 'surplus ethnographic material' archived by WebCite® at http://www.webcitation.org/6u0ibTZcf (last accessed 14 September 2017).
15. The project was published in a small book (Drazin *et al.*, 2013), which can also be accessed online: http://www.materialworldblog.com/occasional/properties-and-social-imagination/ (last accessed 31 October, 2017). UCL Museums and Collections has been at the forefront of experimenting with new ways of working with objects in both teaching and research, with projects on: touch- and object-based learning; bringing collections into health care and well-being settings; and digital mediation, including social cataloguing projects and explorations of the powers of 3D imaging. Some of this research is presented in Chatterjee (2008) and Chatterjee and Hannan (2015). See also Were and King (2012).
16. In Ingold's initial argument (2007) he exhorted readers to wet a stone and lay it by them as they read, observing its transformation over the course of his argument.
17. Currin (2013: 44–50).
18. Küchler (2013: 42–3). This has been widely discussed in the ethnography; see, for instance, Veys (2017).
19. A recent UCL Masters student in material and visual culture, Jasmine Popper, undertook a research project on the concept of the fragment, using a series of broken and decomposing objects to show how the collection challenges the conventional ways in which we understand and categorise objects themselves. See http://tinyurl.com/uclbits (last accessed: 13 January 2017). There have been several recent studies of decay in relations to museum and conservation (e.g. DeSilvey (2017) and Domínguez Rubio (2014, 2016), which focus on the generative capacities of decay to create new ideas about the form of collections and their management.
20. See Fiedorek (2015) for a discussion of the early history of lantern-slides.
21. http://www.carolinewright.com/portfolio/sawdust-and-threads/ (last accessed 31 October 2017).
22. Fowles argues that this comes at a time when anthropology has been increasingly disempowered from representing its traditional subjects the stereotypical anthropological other, all too often defined through processes of colonialism. Fowles (2016); see also Latour (1993) and Lamb (2011) on the silencing, or voice, of things.
23. Dourish (2016).
24. Gibson (1986: 127–43).

Chapter 4

1. For example, Nicholas Thomas' book *Possessions* (1999) describes the ways in which Māori and Aboriginal imagery and motifs were built into the nation-making practices of Australia and New Zealand through the decorative arts and design.
2. Harris (1981), Poignant (2004).
3. My history of the Cooper Hewitt has largely been gleaned from Lynes (1981).
4. McCarty (2014: 27).
5. Lynes (1981: 23).
6. Lynes (1981: 26).
7. See Hinsley and Wilcox (2016), Gere (1998), Greenhalgh (1990), Harvey (1996).

8. Lynes (1981: 34).
9. Robb (2015: 169); see also e.g. Gell (1998) and Ingold (2007).
10. Ruskin's influential criticism in *The Stones of Venice* 2003[1853] and *The Political Economy of Art* (1868) was a searing critique of the industrial revolution and its impact on craft and creative spirit. See also Thompson and Lindebaugh 's biography of William Morris (2011).
11. Barringer (1998: 359).
12. Barringer (2006: 135); see also Bryant (2012).
13. Trask (2006: 2), published in book form as Trask (2013).
14. See e.g. Farrelly and Weddell (2016).
15. Trask (2006: 253).
16. See, for example, Zorach and Rodini (2005), Frederiksen and Marchand (2010), Edwards (2001, 2009, 2012).
17. http://www.vam.ac.uk/content/articles/t/the-cast-courts/ (last accessed 31 October 2017).
18. A similar discourse may be found in the efforts of the *Million Images* database to collect digital images of cultural heritage under threat in the Middle East Region, or in the Europeana database ('a European digital library for all'), which was founded by the European Commission to make Europe's cultural heritage accessible for all. See www.europeana.eu; http://www.millionimage.org.uk (last accessed 31 October 2017).
19. Gombrich (1986), eminent art historian and subsequent director of the Warburg Institute, has written a succinct intellectual biography of Warburg.
20. Gombrich (1986: 283).
21. Gombrich (1986: 284).
22. Quoted in Gombrich (1986: 303).
23. See Johnson (2012), Michaud (2004).
24. Malraux (1967).
25. See Farrelly and Weddell (2016).
26. https://www.cooperhewitt.org/events/current-exhibitions/process-lab/ (last accessed 2 September 2017).
27. Fernando Domínguez Rubio (2014) explores the tensions that so-called new media and time-based media pose for the proprietary art museum, in his case the Museum of Modern Art in New York, struggling to make sense of an artwork that depended on now-obsolete technology: *Untitled* by Nam June Paik.
28. See for example Dudley (2012).
29. The case is discussed in depth by V&A curator Jana Scholze (2016), and by Victor Buchli (2015: 161–75).
30. Wilson tracks his journey to develop the gun, including the tensions between the FBI, government firearms regulators and international computer hackers in his memoir, *Come and Take It: The gun printer's guide to thinking free* (2016).
31. Altshuler (2013) discusses the issues that emerge around collecting 'the new' in contemporary art museums. See also Laurenson *et al.* (2014), Buchli (2010).
32. This has been critiqued by many, including Bourriaud (2002), Bishop (2014) and Domínguez Rubio (2016).
33. See, for example, the ways in which the Museum of Modern Art displays its collection of Apple products as aesthetic artefacts of design or the ways in which it presents its acquisition of the ampersand. In a blog post discussing the acquisition, design curator Paola Antonelli notes that museums rely 'on the assumption that physical possession of an object as a requirement for an acquisition is no longer necessary, and therefore it sets curators free to tag the world and acknowledge things that "cannot be had" – because they are too big (buildings, Boeing 747s, satellites), or because they are in the air and belong to everybody and to no one, like the @ – as art objects befitting MoMA's collection. The same criteria of quality, relevance, and overall excellence shared by all objects in MoMA's collection also apply to these entities' (Antonelli, 2010). Yet as Dominguez Rubio notes, the Museum of Modern Art's role in consolidating the relationship between ownership, authenticity and property that underpins modernist theories of art makes it difficult for the museum to frame its collections in these alternative registers rather than reinforcing existing modes of object-ness and ownership (Domínguez Rubio, 2014).
34. The Cooper Hewitt was one of the first museums to put its collections data into the digital code repository GitHub. This allows people not just to search data, but to access the data itself.
35. Chan and Cope (2015: 336).
36. Parry (2013); see Chan and Cope (2014, 2015).

37. Chan and Cope (2015).
38. Chan and Cope (2015: 355).
39. Chan and Cope (2015: 364).
40. http://www.cooperhewitt.org/2015/03/05/using-the-pen/ (last accessed 31 October 2017).
41. Cara McCarty explicitly describes the contemporary collection strategy as 'user-centered', in which new media becomes a model for a 'playful' approach to the collection (both democratising accessibility and reflecting a theory of design genius), and facilitating what she also terms 'ingenious storytelling' (2014: 31).

Chapter 5

1. Cameron (2008: 229).
2. The names used for 'ethnographic museums' indicates this complexity – within larger encyclopaedic museums, such collections are bracketed geographically in departments of 'Africa, Oceania and the Americas' (for instance, at the Metropolitan Museum of Art, the British Museum), or defined as 'world cultures' (in Frankfurt, Amsterdam, Berlin). Previously, terms such as Museums of Mankind, of Arts Premiers, of Primitive Art and of Indigenous Art also bracketed these collections. The Musée du quai Branly in Paris struggled so much with its name it ended up named after its location. All of these struggles with nomenclature indicate the unsettled ways in which colonial power has structured the naming and classification of so-called 'world culture'.
3. The display is an object lesson about object lessons. The labels are formulated as a series of answered questions (What is it made of? How was it made? When was it made? Where is it from? What does it look like? What else do you notice about it? What is it? What can this object tell us about a person's relation to others, to the natural world, to the supernatural world and how the worlds are integrated?). The answers to these focused on each object are united by a central text: 'Learning through objects: Detailed study of objects provides a wealth of information about culture and human relationships. Integrating that information into a view of what the object reveals is called interpretation. The two objects and the interpretations that are featured here illustrate that concept.' (Label text courtesy of Sarah Hatcher, Head of Education and Programs, Mathers Museum, Indiana University).
4. See for example, Clifford's (1981) discussion of the ways in which juxtaposition contributes to the modernist vision of the primitive other through an act of 'ethnographic surrealism' in twentieth-century ethnographic display.
5. See Price (2007), Clifford (2007). Similar conversations have occurred around the Weltkulturen Museum in Frankfurt (see Geismar, 2015a) and the Humboldt Forum in Berlin (see Macdonald 2015, 2016).
6. Heller *et al.* (2015) summarise the many different projects that were undertaken in this experimental phase of the project.
7. For example, see Bynum (2015) and a special issue of the *Journal of Material Culture* that focuses on the materiality affectivity of bones and human remains, Krmpotich *et al.* (2010) and Renshaw (2010).
8. As Susanne Küchler notes with regard to the complex funerary carvings of New Ireland: 'What Malanggan, bodies, and land share is, firstly, that they are a container, secondly, that the container and the contained – the object and its image, the bones and the skin, the cultivated and settled land – can, and even must, be separated; and thirdly, that the method of separation is an incremental part of the thing itself, as it resonates in its looks, its feel, its smell or its taste' (Küchler, 2002: 169).
9. Note of provenance from the dealer from whom the collector purchased the rambaramp, spellings as in the original (source: Archives of the Department of Africa, Oceania and the Americas at the Metropolitan Museum, object accession number 2000.615. Accessed October 2015).
10. The history of museum collecting in Vanuatu is documented in Speiser (1996), Bonnemaison *et al.* (1996), O'Hanlon and Welsch (2000), Geismar and Herle (2010) and Bolton (2003).
11. See Godelier and Strathern (1991), Geismar (2005), Allen (1981).
12. Susanne Küchler has written extensively about this in her work on Malanggan from New Ireland (see e.g. 1987). For the Asmat region, see Stanley (2012), Jacobs (2011).
13. Küchler (2002: 1).

14. Correspondence between the Met Museum and the Vanuatu Kaljoral Senta, an emailed list of questions (11 March 2002). Correspondence pertaining to 2000.615 (source: Archives of the Department of Africa, Oceania and the Americas at the Metropolitan Museum, object accession number 2000.615, last accessed: October 2015).
15. See Bolton (2003), Geismar and Tilley (2003), Taylor and Thieberger (2011) for accounts of the collaborative infrastructure for ethnographic, archaeological and linguistic research established at the Vanuatu Cultural Centre over many decades.
16. Hugo DeBlock reports in his PhD dissertation that Tessa Fowler, probably the Mrs Tesa referred to above, told him during his fieldwork that due to such high demand in the collectors' market for rambaramp, she imported skulls from a friend who collected war memorabilia from Vietnam to be used in the almost cottage industry she had going in South Malakula. He writes: 'They were posted to Tessa by her friend, and she took them to Malakula in her bag, with food and camping equipment. She did not have to pay duty on the skulls because they were declared for customs as "used skulls" and anything "used" was exempt from duty. Before she had access to these skulls, she added, her small nambas connections went fossicking on burial grounds on Malakula for "used skulls".' (2013: 8).
17. See http://www.metmuseum.org/press/news/2008/three-spectacular-vases-lent-by-italy-to-metropolitan-museum-for-four-years-replace-euphronios-krater and http://traffickingculture.org/encyclopedia/case-studies/euphronios-sarpedon-krater/ (last accessed 13 January 2017).
18. T. Bennett (1995, 2004).
19. See Holbraad and Pederson (2017), Holbraad *et al.* (2016), Alberti *et al.* (2011), Graeber (2015).
20. See e.g. Viveiros de Castro (1998). A recent essay by David Graeber (2015) exposes the conceptual inadequacies of these arguments in which the very conception of incommensurable multiple worlds is produced from the singularising perspective of the academic analyst, who ventroliquises the native 'perspective' in much the same way as the Totem's Sound app as discussed earlier in this chapter.
21. Moutu (2007: 100).
22. Harrison *et al.* (2013) explore ethnographic collections explicitly in terms of assemblages, unravelling the determinism of ethnographic categories in order to create space for Indigenous interpretation and agency.
23. This definition underpins Miller's articulation of materiality (2005).
24. See Castells (2000), Lessig (2006), Boyle (1996).
25. Kelty (2008).
26. Geismar (2012, 2013a, 2016).
27. See www.irititja.com, www.mukurtu.org. e.g. Verran and Christie (2014).
28. I discuss the relationship between the relational database and other formulations of relation-making in Geismar and Mohns (2011).
29. This is based on the site at the time of writing, 1 March 2016, which incidentally marks a beta relaunch of the website with the goal of making the site better suited to mobile experience, a better integration of the museum's multiple physical locations, and a better encapsulation of the museum's institutional identity.
30. Wilson (2011: 380).
31. Wilson (2011: 386).
32. Bowker and Star (2000).
33. Rio (2002) and Godelier and Strathern (1991), for instance, have documented the ethnographic complexity of the ritual systems of this region.
34. See Geismar (2005, 2009a).
35. Boast and Enote (2013: 110); see also the edited collection focused on digital return by Bell *et al.* (2013).
36. https://www.youtube.com/watch?feature=player_embedded&v=9KiVNIUMmCc (last accessed 31 October 2017).
37. Echoing Baxandall's articulation of a 'period eye' (1988).
38. Heidegger (1977), Baxandall (1988).
39. I take some of this text from a review I wrote previously of the exhibition, published on http://www.materialworldblog.com/2014/06/technology-and-knowing-at-the-british-museum/. See this interactive video for a full experience of the exhibition: https://www.theguardian.com/artanddesign/video/2014/may/19/ancient-lives-british-museum-mummification-padiamenet-video (last accessed 31 October 2017).

Chapter 6

1. A shorter version of this chapter was published in Geismar (2015b). For those who are not familiar with Te Reo Māori (the Māori language), the following glossary of words that are used frequently here, and which emerged as part of the project as a conceptual framework, might be a helpful reference point when reading the chapter. I take these definitions from www.maoridictionary.co.nz, an online dictionary produced by Te Whanake, Māori Language Online)

   Kaitiaki – (noun) trustee, minder, guard, custodian, guardian, caregiver, keeper, steward.

   Kaupapa – (noun) topic, policy, matter for discussion, plan, purpose, scheme, proposal, agenda, subject, programme, theme, issue, initiative. Also the name used to refer to the main body of a cloak.

   Koha – (noun) gift, present, offering, donation, contribution – especially one maintaining social relationships and has connotations of reciprocity.

   Marae – (noun) courtyard – the open area in front of the *wharenui* (meeting house) where formal greetings and discussions take place. Often also used to include the complex of buildings around the *marae*. Also used as a verb to mean to be generous, hospitable.

   Mihi – (noun) speech of greeting, acknowledgement, tribute.

   Powhiri – (noun) invitation, rituals of encounter, welcome ceremony on a marae, welcome.

   Taonga – (noun) treasure, anything prized – applied to anything considered to be of value, including socially or culturally valuable objects, resources, phenomena, ideas and techniques.

   Wairua – (noun) spirit, soul – spirit of a person that exists beyond death. It is the non-physical spirit, distinct from the body AND (noun) attitude, quintessence, feel, mood, feeling, nature, essence, atmosphere.

   Whakapapa – (noun) genealogy, genealogical table, lineage, descent – reciting *whakapapa* was, and is, an important skill and reflected the importance of genealogies in Māori society in terms of leadership, land and fishing rights, kinship and status. It is central to all Māori institutions.

2. See Pearce (1990).
3. Hoskins (1998), Cruikshank (2000), Tilley (1999), Kopytoff (1986).
4. Following Māori custom, cloaks, as ancestral *taonga*, or treasures, are always female.
5. Geismar (2013b), Henare (2005b, 2007), Salmond (1997), Tapsell (1997, 2006, 2017).
6. See Metge (2010).
7. I discuss this in a special web issue of cultural anthropology, which asked if there was an ontology to the digital, Geismar (2016).
8. Chris Pinney (2008) has argued that this is part of the power of still photography as well, so this capacity of media to capture more than the eye can see is by no means unique to the digital.
9. See Macdonald *et al.* (2012).
10. E.g. Hess *et al.* (2011, 2015).
11. E.g. see Hess *et al.* (2015).
12. Anderson (2011), Rader and Cain (2014) and Haraway (1984) discuss the history and aesthetics of natural history display technologies.
13. Mitchell (1996).
14. Tapsell (1997).
15. Mead (1990, 2003).
16. Salmond (2013: 15).
17. E.g. Guss (1989), Mackenzie (1991) and Were (2013) talk about the entanglement of the weaving processes and materials and the constitution of social relationships in different contexts in Amazonia and Melanesia respectively.
18. Henare (2005b).
19. E.g. Tapsell (2000), Schorch and Hakiwai (2014), Smith (2008), Baker (2008), Ngata *et al.* (2012).

Conclusion

1. *Bears on Stairs* is a digital animation that has been produced from 3D-printed objects, developed from digital renderings, presenting the digital as continually nested within analogue materiality and vice versa. I thank Zoe Laughlin for drawing my attention to this project.
2. Parry (2013).
3. Marres (2012: 27).
4. Crary (1999), Kenderdine (2016).
5. Mitchell (2002, 2005) critiques the limited purview of 'visual studies', arguing that 'that there are no visual media'.
6. Taussig (1993: xiii).
7. See Quinn (2006) for a broader exposition about the art of dioramas. 'The okapi diorama holds a secret unknown to most visitors. Foreground artist George Frederick Mason collaborated with James Perry Wilson on this diorama, and knowing how Wilson loved riddles and puzzles, Mason painted a hidden chipmunk into the background painting and challenged Wilson to find it. The whimsical little creation remains in the background today, scampering across the African forest floor in full view of the public.' (http://tumblr.amnh.org/post/114403305329/the-okapi-diorama-holds-a-secret-unknown-to-most, last accessed: 5 October 2017).
8. Dahl (2016 [1964]).
9. Clammer (2016).
10. See http://nellesalbadri.com (last accessed: 14 September 2017).
11. See Wilder (2016a) for coverage of the project; the video of the artists' hack can be found here: https://vimeo.com/148156899 (last accessed: 6 October 2017).
12. The Actuality of the Ancient: Contemporary Art, Icons and Identity, 30 November 2015, documented on YouTube: https://www.youtube.com/watch?v=VlDOt4d9moU (last accessed 15 December 2018). See also the artists' catalogue, Al Badri and Nelles (2017).
13. See David Gill's comment on his blog, Looting Matters: (http://lootingmatters.blogspot.co.uk/2009/12/nefertiti-hawass-plans-action.html) for commentary on the claims by Zahi Hawass on behalf of the government of Egypt that the bust was illegally acquired and should be returned to Egypt.
14. See Newitz (2016), Wilder (2016b) for sceptical accounts stating that Al-Badri and Nelles used data they had collected themselves, asserting that the hack was in fact a double hack.
15. Taussig (1993: chapter 17).
16. See Ginsburg (2008), Bell *et al.* (2013), Boast and Enote (2013) for some critical perspectives, and Srinivasan *et al.* (2009) for some more celebratory perspective.
17. See Keramidas (2015) on a book and exhibition project to explore personal computing as an interface experience.
18. This quote is taken from Bell *et al.* (2013: final paragraph).

References cited

Al-Badri, Nora, and Jan Nikolai Nelles. 2017. *Not a Single Bone*. Berlin: NOME Gallery.

Alberti, Benjamin, Severin Fowles, Martin Holbraad, Yvonne Marshall and Christopher Witmore. 2011. '"Worlds Otherwise": Archaeology, Anthropology, and Ontological Difference.' *Current Anthropology* 52 (6): 896–912. doi:10.1086/662027.

Alberti, Samuel J.M.M., and Elizabeth Hallam, eds. 2013. *Medical Museums: Past, Present, Future*. London: The Royal College of Surgeons of England.

Allen, Michael. 1981. *Vanuatu: Politics, Economics and Ritual in Island Melanesia*. Academic Press: Sydney.

Altshuler, Bruce, ed. 2013. *Collecting the New: Museums and Contemporary Art*. Princeton: Princeton University Press.

Anderson, Jane. 2012. 'Options for the Future Protection of GRTKTCEs: The Traditional Knowledge Licenses and Labels Initiative.' *Journal of the World Intellectual Property Organization* 4 (1): 73–82.

Anderson, Jane, and Kimberly Christen. 2013. '"Chuck a Copyright on It": Dilemmas of Digital Return and the Possibilities for Traditional Knowledge Licenses and Labels.' *Museum Anthropology Review* 7 (1–2): 105–26.

Anderson, Michael. 2011. 'Painting Actuality: Diorama Art of James Perry Wilson.' 28 September. http://peabody.yale.edu/james-perry-wilson. Last accessed: 1 September 2017.

Antonelli, Paola. 2010. '@ at MoMA.' *Inside/Out: A MoMA/MoMA PS1 Blog*. 22 March. https://www.moma.org/explore/inside_out/2010/03/22/at-moma/. Last accessed: 1 September 2017.

Appadurai, Arjun, ed. 1988. *The Social Life of Things: Commodities in Cultural Perspective*. Cambridge and New York: Cambridge University Press.

Appiah, Kwame Anthony. 2006. *Cosmopolitanism: Ethics in a World of Strangers*. New York: W.W. Norton.

Baker, Jade Tangiahua. 2008. 'Te Pahitaua: Border Negotiators.' *International Journal of Cultural Property* 15 (2): 141. https://doi.org/10.1017/S0940739108080120.

Bakke, Gretchen Anna. 2016. *The Grid: The Fraying Wires between Americans and Our Energy Future*. New York: Bloomsbury USA.

Barney, Darin, Gabriella Coleman, Christina Ross, Jonathan Sterne and Tamar Tembeck, eds. 2016. *The Participatory Condition in the Digital Age*. Electronic Mediations 51. Minneapolis: University of Minnesota Press.

Barringer, Tim. 1998. 'Re-presenting the Imperial Archive: South Kensington and Its Museums.' *Journal of Victorian Culture* 3 (2): 357–73.

———. 2006. 'Victorian Culture and the Museum: Before and after the White Cube.' *Journal of Victorian Culture* 11 (1): 133–45.

Barringer, Tim, and Tom Flynn, eds. 1998. *Colonialism and the Object: Empire, Material Culture and the Museum*. London and New York: Routledge.

Barry, Andrew. 2013. *Material Politics: Disputes along the Pipeline*. Chichester, West Sussex: Wiley-Blackwell.

Baxandall, Michael. 1988. *Painting and Experience in Fifteenth-Century Italy: A Primer in the Social History of Pictorial Style*. 2nd ed. Oxford and New York: Oxford University Press.

Bell, Joshua A., Kimberly A. Christen and Mark Turin. 2013. 'Introduction: After the Return.' *Museum Anthropology Review* 7 (1–2): 1–21.

Bennett, Jane. 2010. *Vibrant Matter: A Political Ecology of Things*. Durham, N.C.: Duke University Press.

Bennett, Tony. 1988. 'The Exhibitionary Complex.' *New Formations* 4 (1): 73–102.

———. 1995. *The Birth of the Museum: History, Theory, Politics*. London and New York: Routledge.

———. 2004. *Pasts beyond Memory: Evolution, Museums, Colonialism*. Oxon; New York: Routledge.

Bennett, Tony, Fiona Cameron, Nelia Das, Ben Dibley, Rodney Harrison, Ira Jacknis and Conal McCarthy. 2017. *Collecting, Ordering, Governing: Anthropology, Museums, and Liberal Government*. Durham, N.C.: Duke University Press.

Bishop, Claire. 2014. *Radical Museology, or What's 'Contemporary' in Museums of Contemporary Art?* 2nd ed. London: Koenig Books.

Blanchette, Jean-François. 2011. 'A Material History of Bits.' *Journal of the American Society for Information Science and Technology* 62 (6): 1042–57. doi:10.1002/asi.21542.

Boas, Franz. 1887. 'Museums of Ethnology and Their Classification.' *Science* 9 (228): 587–9.

———. 1907. 'Some Principles of Museum Administration.' *Science* 25 (650): 921–33.

Boast, Robin. 2011. 'Neocolonial Collaboration: Museum as Contact Zone Revisited.' *Museum Anthropology* 34 (1): 56–70. doi:10.1111/j.1548-1379.2010.01107.x.

Boast, Robin, and Jim Enote. 2013. 'Virtual Repatriation: It Is Neither Virtual nor Repatriation.' In *Heritage in the Context of Globalization: Europe and the Americas*, edited by Peter F. Biehl and Christopher Prescott, 103–13. New York, NY: Springer New York.

Boellstorff, Tom. 2016. 'For Whom the Ontology Turns: Theorizing the Digital Real.' *Current Anthropology* 57 (4): 387–407. doi:10.1086/687362.

Bolton, Lissant. 2003. *Unfolding the Moon: Enacting Women's Kastom in Vanuatu*. Honolulu: University of Hawaii Press.

Bonnemaison, Joel, Kirk Huffman, Christian Kaufmann and Darrell Tryon. 1996. *Arts of Vanuatu*. Bathurst: Crawford House Publishing.

Bourriaud, Nicolas. 2002. *Relational Aesthetics*. Paris: Les Presses du Réel.

Bowker, Geoffrey C., and Susan Leigh Star. 2000. *Sorting Things Out: Classification and Its Consequences*. Cambridge, Mass.: MIT Press.

Boylan, Patrick. 2006. 'The Museum Profession.' In *A Companion to Museum Studies*, edited by Sharon Macdonald, 415–30. Blackwell Companions in Cultural Studies 12. Malden, MA: Blackwell.

Boyle, James. 1996. *Shamans, Software, and Spleens: Law and the Construction of the Information Society*. Cambridge, Mass.: Harvard University Press.

Briggs, Asa. 1988. *Victorian Things*. 1st ed. London: B.T. Batsford Ltd.

Brown, Alison K., and Laura Peers. 2013. 'The Blackfoot Shirts Project: "Our Ancestors Have Come to Visit."' In *The International Handbooks of Museum Studies*, edited by Sharon Macdonald and Helen Rees Leahy, 263–87. Oxford: John Wiley & Sons, Ltd.

Brown, Bill. 2001. 'Thing Theory.' *Critical Inquiry* 28 (1): 1–22. https://doi.org/10.1086/449030.

Brown, Deirdre. 2007. 'Te Ahu Hiko: Digital Cultural Heritage and Indigenous Objects, People and Environments.' In *Theorizing Digital Cultural Heritage: A Critical Discourse*, edited by Fiona Cameron and Sarah Kenderdine, 77–93. Cambridge, Massachusetts and London, England: The MIT Press.

Brown, Michael F. 2003. *Who Owns Native Culture?* Cambridge, Mass.: Harvard University Press.

Bryant, Julius, ed. 2012. *Art and Design for All: The Victoria and Albert Museum*. South Kensington, London: V & A Publishing.

Buchli, Victor. 2010. 'The Prototype: Presencing the Immaterial.' *Visual Communication* 9 (3): 273–86. doi:10.1177/1470357210372718.

———. 2015. *An Archaeology of the Immaterial*. London and New York: Routledge.

Bynum, Caroline Walker. 2015. *Christian Materiality: An Essay on Religion in Late Medieval Europe*. Brooklyn, NY: MIT Press.

Cameron, Fiona. 2008. 'Object-Oriented Democracies: Conceptualising Museum Collections in Networks.' *Museum Management and Curatorship* 23 (3): 229–43. https://doi.org/10.1080/09647770802233807.

Candlin, Fiona. 2015. *Micromuseology*. London and New York: Bloomsbury Academic.

Carvajal, Doreen. 2017. 'Let a robot be your museum tour guide.' *The New York Times*: Art and Design Section, 14 March 2017. https://www.nytimes.com/2017/03/14/arts/design/museums-experiment-with-robots-as-guides.html (last accessed 9 November 2017).

Castells, Manuel. 2000. *The Rise of the Network Society: The Information Age: Economy, Society and Culture*. Oxford: John Wiley & Sons, Ltd.

Chalker, Kari, Lois Sherr Dubin, Peter M. Whiteley and American Museum of Natural History, eds. 2004. *Totems to Turquoise: Native North American Jewelry Arts of the Northwest and Southwest*. New York: Harry N. Abrams: In association with the American Museum of Natural History.

Chan, Sebastian. 2015. 'Strategies against Architecture: Interactive Media and Transformative Technology at Cooper Hewitt.' *MW2015: Museums and the Web 2015*. 6 April. http://mw2015.museumsandtheweb.com/paper/strategies-against-architecture-interactive-media-and-transformative-technology-at-cooper-hewitt/ (last accessed: 11 September 2017).

Chan, Sebastian, and Aaron Cope. 2014. 'Collecting the Present: Digital Code and Collections.' *MW2014: Museums and the Web 2014*. 19 March. http://mw2014.museumsandtheweb.com/paper/collecting-the-present-digital-code-and-collections/ (last accessed: 11 September 2017).

Chatterjee, Helen. 2008. *Touch in Museums: Policy and Practice in Object Handling*. Oxford and New York: Bloomsbury Academic.

Chatterjee, Helen J., and Leonie Hannan, eds. 2015. *Engaging the Senses: Object-Based Learning in Higher Education*. Farnham, Surrey; Burlington, VT: Ashgate.

Christen, Kimberly. 2005. 'Gone Digital: Aboriginal Remix and the Cultural Commons.' *International Journal of Cultural Property* 12 (3): 315. doi:10.1017/S0940739105050186.

———. 2011. 'Opening Archives: Respectful Repatriation.' *American Archivist* 74 (1): 185–210.

———. 2012. 'Does Information Really Want to be Free? Indigenous Knowledge Systems and the Question of Openness.' *International Journal of Communication* [S.l.] 6 (Nov): 24. ISSN 1932-8036. Available at: http://ijoc.org/index.php/ijoc/article/view/1618. (Last accessed: 7 November 2017).

Christie, Michael, and Helen Verran. 2013. 'Digital Lives in Postcolonial Aboriginal Australia.' *Journal of Material Culture* 18 (3): 299–317. doi:10.1177/1359183513492081.

Clammer, Paul. 2016. 'Erasing Isis: how 3D technology now lets us copy and rebuild entire cities.' *The Guardian*: Cities Section, 27 May 2016. https://www.theguardian.com/cities/2016/may/27/isis-palmyra-3d-technology-copy-rebuild-city-venice-biennale (last accessed 21 October 2017).

Clifford, James. 1981. 'On Ethnographic Surrealism.' *Comparative Studies in Society and History* 23 (4): 539–64.

———. 1988. *The Predicament of Culture: Twentieth-Century Ethnography, Literature, and Art*. Cambridge, Mass.: Harvard University Press.

———. 1997. 'Museums as Contact Zones.' In *Routes: Travel and Translation in the Late Twentieth Century*, 188–220. Cambridge, Mass.: Harvard University Press.

———. 2007. 'Quai Branly in Process.' *October* (spring): 3–23. https://doi.org/10.1162/octo.2007.120.1.3.

Coleman, E. Gabriella. 2012. *Coding Freedom: The Ethics and Aesthetics of Hacking*. Princeton: Princeton University Press.

Conn, Steven. 1998. *Museums and American Intellectual Life, 1876–1926*. Chicago: Chicago University Press.

———. 2010. *Do Museums Still Need Objects?* Philadelphia: University of Pennsylvania Press.

Connolly, William E. 2013. 'The "New Materialism" and the Fragility of Things.' *Millennium* 41 (3): 399–412. doi:10.1177/0305829813486849.

Coole, Diana H., and Samantha Frost, eds. 2010. *New Materialisms: Ontology, Agency, and Politics*. Durham, N.C.; London: Duke University Press.

Coombes, Annie E. 1997. *Reinventing Africa: Museums, Material Culture and Popular Imagination in Late Victorian and Edwardian England*. New Haven, CT: Yale University Press.

Corrin, Lisa G. 1994. *Mining the Museum: An Installation*. Baltimore; New York: New Press: Contemporary; W.W. Norton.

Costa, Elisabetta, Nell Haynes, Tom Mcdonald, Daniel Miller, Razvan Nicolescu, Jolynna Sinanan, Juliano Spyer, Shriram Venkatraman and Xinyuan Wang. 2016. *How the World Changed Social Media*. London: UCL Press. https://www.ucl.ac.uk/ucl-press/browse-books/how-world-changed-social-media (last accessed 8 January 2018).

Coupaye, Ludovic. 2013. *Growing Artefacts, Displaying Relationships: Yams, Art and Technology Amongst the Nyamikum Abelam of Papua New Guinea*. New York: Berghahn Books.

Crary, Jonathan. 1999. *Suspensions of Perception: Attention, Spectacle, and Modern Culture*. Cambridge, Mass.: MIT Press.

Cruikshank, Julie. 2000. *The Social Life of Stories: Narrative & Knowledge in the Yukon Territory: Narrative and Knowledge in the Yukon Territory*. Lincoln: Bison.

Currin, Katherine. 2013. 'Analysis of Volatiles Emitted from Barkcloth.' In *Properties and Social Imagination*, edited by Adam Drazin, Haidy Geismar and Camilla Sundwall, 44–49. UCL Anthropology: Material World Occasional Paper 4.

Cuno, James B. 2008. *Who Owns Antiquity? Museums and the Battle over Our Ancient Heritage*. Princeton, N.J.; Woodstock: Princeton University Press.

———. 2009. *Whose Culture? The Promise of Museums and the Debate over Antiquities*. Princeton, N.J. and Oxford: Princeton University Press.

Dahl, Roald. 2016. *Charlie and the Chocolate Factory*. London: Puffin Press.

Daston, Lorraine. 2007. 'Speechless.' In *Things That Talk: Object Lessons from Art and Science*, edited by Lorraine Daston, 9–24. New York: Zone Books.

DeBlock, Hugo. 2013. 'Artifak: The Commoditization, Valuation and Authentication of (Art) Objects in Vanuatu, South West Pacific.' PhD, Melbourne, Australia: University of Melbourne.

Deger, Jennifer. 2006. *Shimmering Screens: Making Media in an Aboriginal Community*. Vol. 19. Minneapolis: University of Minnesota Press.

———. 2008. 'Imprinting on the Heart: Photography and Contemporary Yolngu Mournings.' *Visual Anthropology* 21 (4): 292–309. doi:10.1080/08949460802156318.

———. 2016. 'Thick Photography.' *Journal of Material Culture* 21 (1): 111–32. doi:10.1177/1359183515623312.

DeSilvey, Caitlin. 2017. *Curated Decay: Heritage beyond Saving*. Minneapolis: University of Minnesota Press.

Domínguez Rubio, Fernando. 2014. 'Preserving the Unpreservable: Docile and Unruly Objects at MoMA.' *Theory and Society* 43 (6): 617–45. doi:10.1007/s11186-014-9233-4.

———. 2016. 'On the Discrepancy between Objects and Things: An Ecological Approach.' *Journal of Material Culture* 21 (1): 59–86. doi:10.1177/1359183515624128.

Dourish, Paul. 2016. 'Rematerializing the Platform: Emulation and the Digital-Material.' In *Digital Materialities: Design and Anthropology*, edited by Sarah Pink, Elisenda Ardèvol and Dèbora Lanzeni, 29–44. London and New York: Bloomsbury Academic.

Drazin, Adam. 2015. 'Introduction: To Live in a Materials World.' In *The Social Life of Materials*, edited by Adam Drazin and Susanne Küchler, 3–28. London and New York: Bloomsbury Academic.

Drazin, Adam, Haidy Geismar and Camilla Sundwall, eds. 2013. *Properties and Social Imagination*. UCL Anthropology: Material World Occasional Paper 4.

Drazin, Adam, and Susanne Küchler, eds. 2015. *The Social Life of Materials*. London; New York: Bloomsbury Academic.

Dudley, Sandra H. 2012. 'Encountering a Chinese Horse: Engaging with the Thingness of Things.' In *Museum Objects: Experiencing the Properties of Things*, edited by Sandra H. Dudley, 1–17. Leicester Readers in Museum Studies. London; New York, NY: Routledge.

———, ed. 2012 *Museum Objects: Experiencing the Properties of Things*. Leicester Readers in Museum Studies. London and New York, NY: Routledge.

Edwards, Elizabeth. 2001. *Raw Histories: Photographs, Anthropology and Museums*. 1st ed. London and New York: Bloomsbury Academic.

———. 2009. 'Unblushing Realism and the Threat of the Pictorial: Photographic Survey and the Production of Evidence 1885–1918.' *History of Photography* 33 (1): 3–17. doi: 10.1080/03087290802586153.

———. 2012. *The Camera as Historian: Amateur Photographers and Historical Imagination, 1885–1918*. Durham, N.C.: Duke University Press.

Edwards, Elizabeth, Chris Gosden and Ruth B. Phillips. 2006. *Sensible Objects: Colonialism, Museums and Material Culture*. Oxford and New York: Berg.

Evens, Aden. 2012. 'Web 2.0 and the Ontology of the Digital.' *Digital Humanities Quarterly* 6 (2). Available at: http://www.digitalhumanities.org/dhq/vol/6/2/000120/000120.html. (last accessed 20 November 2016).

Farrelly, Liz, and Joanna Weddell, eds. 2016. *Design Objects and the Museum*. London and New York: Bloomsbury Academic.

Fenton, James. 1984. 'The Pitt Rivers Museum, Oxford.' *Newsletter (Museum Ethnographers Group)* 16 (April): 37–40.

Fiedorek, Kara. 2015. 'Varieties of Photographic Experience: Frederick H. Evans and the Lantern Slide.' *British Art Studies* 1 (November). doi:10.17658/issn.2058-5462/issue-01/kfiedorek.

Findlen, Paula. 1996. *Possessing Nature: Museums, Collecting, and Scientific Culture in Early Modern Italy*. Berkeley: University of California Press.

Fish, Adam. 2017. *Technoliberalism and the End of Participatory Culture in the United States*. Houndsmills, Basingstoke, Hampshire; New York Palgrave Macmillan.

Fowles, Severin. 2016. 'The Perfect Subject (Postcolonial Object Studies).' *Journal of Material Culture* 21 (1): 9–27. doi:10.1177/1359183515623818.

Fraser, Andrea. 2007. *Museum Highlights: The Writings of Andrea Fraser*. Cambridge, Mass.: MIT Press.

Frederiksen, Rune, and Eckart Marchand. 2010. *Plaster Casts: Making, Collecting and Displaying from Classical Antiquity to the Present*. Berlin: Walter de Gruyter.

Gabrys, Jennifer. 2011. *Digital Rubbish: A Natural History of Electronics*. Ann Arbor, Michigan: University of Michigan Press.

Geismar, Haidy. 2005. 'Copyright in Context: Carvings, Carvers, and Commodities in Vanuatu.' *American Ethnologist* 32 (3): 437–59. doi:10.1525/ae.2005.32.3.437.

———. 2008. 'Cultural Property, Museums, and the Pacific: Reframing the Debates.' *International Journal of Cultural Property* 15 (2): 109–22. doi:10.1017/S0940739108080089.

———. 2009a. 'Stone Men of Malekula on Malakula: An Ethnography of an Ethnography.' *Ethnos: Journal of Anthropology* 74 (2): 199–228.

———. 2009b. 'Photographs and Foundations: Visualizing the past on Atchin and Vao.' In *Moving Images: John Layard, Fieldwork and Photography on Malakula since 1914*, Haidy Geismar and Anita Herle, 257–92. Honolulu: Crawford House and the University of Hawai'i Press.

———. 2011. '"Material Culture Studies" and Other Ways to Theorize Objects: A Primer to a Regional Debate.' *Comparative Studies in Society and History* 53 (1): 210–18. doi:10.1017/S001041751000068X.

———. 2012. 'Museum + Digital =?' In *Digital Anthropology*, edited by Heather Horst and Daniel Miller, 277–87 Oxford: Berg Publishers.

———. 2013a. 'Defining the Digital.' *Museum Anthropology Review* 7 (1–2): 254–63.

———. 2013b. *Treasured Possessions: Indigenous Interventions into Cultural and Intellectual Property*. Durham, N.C.: Duke University Press.

———. 2015a. 'The Art of Anthropology: Questioning Contemporary Art in Ethnographic Display.' In *The International Handbooks of Museum Studies: Museum Theory*, edited by Sharon Macdonald, Helen Rees Leahy, Kylie Message and Andrea Witcomb, 1: 183–210. Oxford John Wiley & Sons, Ltd.

———. 2015b. 'Post-Photographic Presences, or How to Wear a Digital Cloak.' *Photographies* 8 (3): 305–21. doi:10.1080/17540763.2015.1102760.

———. 2016. 'A Dissonant Digital Ontology – Cultural Anthropology.' Available at: https://culanth.org/fieldsights/829-a-dissonant-digital-ontology (last accessed 8 January 2018).

Geismar, Haidy, and Anita Herle. 2010. *Moving Images: John Layard, Photography and Fieldwork on Malakula since 1914*. Honolulu: Crawford House and the University of Hawai'i Press.

Geismar, Haidy, and William Mohns. 2011. 'Database Relations: Rethinking the Database in the Vanuatu Cultural Centre and National Museum.' *Journal of the Royal Anthropological Institute* 17 (s1): s133–55.

Geismar, Haidy, and Christopher Tilley. 2003. 'Negotiating Materiality: International and Local Museum Practices at the Vanuatu Cultural Centre and National Museum.' *Oceania* 73 (3): 170–88.

Gell, Alfred. 1998. *Art and Agency: An Anthropological Theory*. Oxford and New York: Clarendon Press; Oxford University Press.

Gerbaudo, Paolo. 2012. *Tweets and the Streets: Social Media and Contemporary Activism*. London: Pluto Press.

Gere, Charlotte. 1998. 'European Decorative Arts at the World Fairs: 1850–1900.' *Metropolitan Museum of Art Bulletin* 56 (3): 3–56.

Gibson, James J. 1986. *The Ecological Approach to Visual Perception*. Boston: Routledge.

Gimblett, Barbara Kirschenblatt. 1991. 'Objects of Ethnography.' In *Exhibiting Cultures: The Poetics and Politics of Museum Display*, edited by Ivan Karp and Steven Lavine, 386–443. Washington, D.C.: Smithsonian Institution Press.

Ginsburg, Faye. 1991. 'Indigenous Media: Faustian Contract or Global Village?' *Cultural Anthropology* 6 (1): 92–112.

———. 2008. 'Rethinking the Digital Age.' In *Global Indigenous Media: Cultures, Poetics, and Politics*, edited by Stewart Wilson and Pamela Michelle, 287–306. Durham, N.C.: Duke University Press.

Gitelman, Lisa. 2006. *Always Already New: Media, History, and the Data of Culture*. Cambridge, Mass.: MIT Press.

Gitelman, Lisa, and Geoffrey B. Pingree, eds. 2004. *New Media, 1740–1915*. Media in Transition Series. Cambridge, Massachusetts and London: MIT Press.

Glass, Aaron. 2009. 'Frozen Poses: Hamat'sa Dioramas, Recursive Representation and the Making of a Kwakwaka'wakw Icon.' In *Photography, Anthropology and History: Expanding the Frame*, edited by Christopher Morton and Elizabeth Edwards, 89–116. Farnham, Surrey, England; Burlington, VT: Ashgate.

———, ed. 2011. *Objects of Exchange: Social and Material Transformation on the Late Nineteenth-Century Northwest Coast: Selections from the American Museum of Natural History*. New York: New Haven: Bard Graduate Center: Decorative Arts, Design History, Material Culture; Distributed by Yale University Press.

———. 2015. 'Indigenous Ontologies, Digital Futures: Plural Provenances and the Kwakwaka'wakw Collection in Berlin and Beyond.' In *Museum as Process: Translating Local and Global Knowledges*, edited by Raymond Silverman, 19–44. Oxford and New York: Routledge.

Godelier, Maurice, and Marilyn Strathern, eds. 1991. *Big Men and Great Men: Personifications of Power in Melanesia*. Cambridge: Cambridge University Press.

Gombrich, Ernst H. 1986. *Aby Warburg: An Intellectual Biography*. 2nd ed. Oxford: Phaidon.

Gosden, Chris, Frances Larsen and Alison Petch. 2007. *Knowing Things: Exploring the Collections at the Pitt Rivers Museum, 1884–1945*. Oxford and New York: Oxford University Press.

Graeber, David. 2015. 'Radical Alterity Is Just Another Way of Saying "reality": A Reply to Eduardo Viveiros de Castro.' *HAU: Journal of Ethnographic Theory* 5 (2): 1–41. doi:10.14318/hau5.2.003.

Graham, Helen. 2016. 'The "Co" in Co-Production: Museums, Community Participation and Science and Technology Studies.' *Science Museum Group Journal* 5 (5). doi:10.15180/160502.

Greenblatt, Stephen. 1991. 'Resonance and Wonder.' In *Exhibiting Cultures: The Poetics and Politics of Museum Display*, 42–56. Washington, D.C.: Smithsonian Institution Press.

Greenhalgh, Paul. 1990. *Ephemeral Vistas: History of the Expositions Universelles, Great Exhibitions and World's Fairs*. Manchester: Manchester University Press.

Griffiths, Alison. 2002. *Wondrous Difference: Cinema, Anthropology, & Turn-of-the-Century Visual Culture*. New York: Columbia University Press.

———. 2008. *Shivers Down Your Spine: Cinema, Museums, and the Immersive View*. Film and Culture. New York: Columbia University Press.

Guss, David M. 1989. *To Weave and Sing: Art, Symbol, and Narrative in the South American Rain Forest*. Berkeley: University of California Press.

Haraway, Donna. 1984. 'Teddy Bear Patriarchy: Taxidermy in the Garden of Eden, New York City, 1908–1936.' *Social Text*, 11 (December): 20–64. doi:10.2307/466593.

Harding, Susan, and Emily Martin. 2016. 'Anthropology Now and Then in the American Museum of Natural History.' *Anthropology Now* 8 (3): 1–13. doi:10.1080/19428200.2016.1242906.

Harris, Neil. 1981. *Humbug: The Art of P. T. Barnum*. Phoenix Ed edition. Chicago: University of Chicago Press.

Harrison, Rodney, Sarah Byrne and Anne Clarke, eds. 2013. *Reassembling the Collection: Ethnographic Museums and Indigenous Agency*. Advanced Seminar Series. Santa Fe: School for Advanced Research Press.

Harvey, Penelope. 1996. *Hybrids of Modernity: Anthropology, the Nation State and the Universal Exhibition*. London: Routledge.

Harvey, Penny, Eleanor Conlin Casella, Gillian Evans, Hannah Knox, Christine McLean, Elizabeth B. Silva, Nicholas Thoburn and Kath Woodward, eds. 2013. *Objects and Materials: A Routledge Companion*. London and New York: Routledge.

Harvey, Penny, and Hannah Knox. 2015. *Roads: An Anthropology of Infrastructure and Expertise*. Ithaca and London: Cornell University Press.

Heidegger, Martin. 1977. 'The Age of the World Picture.' In *The Question Concerning Technology and Other Essays*, Martin Heidegger, 115–55. New York: Harper and Row.

Hein, Hilde S. 2000. *The Museum in Transition: A Philosophical Perspective*. Washington: Smithsonian Institution Press.

Heller, Martin, Andrea Scholz and Agnes Wegner, eds. 2015. *The Laboratory Concept: Museum Experiments in the Humboldt Lab Dahlem*. [Halle an der Saale]: Berlin: Kulturstiftung des Bundes; Nicolai.

Henare, Amiria. 2005a. *Museums, Anthropology and Imperial Exchange*. Cambridge and New York: Cambridge University Press.

———. 2005b. 'Nga Aho Tipuna (Ancestral Threads): Māori Cloaks from New Zealand.' In *Clothing as Material Culture*, edited by Susanne Küchler and Daniel Miller, 121–38. Oxford: Berg.

———. 2007. 'Taonga Māori: Encompassing Rights and Property in New Zealand.' In *Thinking through Things: Theorising Artefacts in Ethnographic Perspective*, edited by Amiria Henare, Martin Holbraad and Sari Wastell, 57–83. London and New York: Routledge.

Henare, Amiria, Martin Holbraad and Sari Wastell, eds. 2007. *Thinking through Things: Theorising Artefacts Ethnographically*. London and New York: Routledge.

Hendry, Joy. 2005. *Reclaiming Culture: Indigenous People and Self-Representation*. Houndsmills, Basingstoke, Hampshire and New York: Palgrave Macmillan.

Henning, Michelle. 2007. 'Legibility and Affect: Museums as New Media.' In *Exhibition Experiments*, 25–47. Oxford: Blackwell.

Hess, Mona, Francesca Simon Millar, Stuart Robson, Sally MacDonald, Graeme Were and Ian Brown. 2011. 'Well Connected to Your Digital Object? E-Curator: A Web-Based E-Science Platform for Museum Artefacts.' *Literary and Linguistic Computing* 26 (2): 193–215. doi:10.1093/llc/fqr006.

Hess, Mona, Stuart Robson, Margaret Serpico, Giancarlo Amati, Ivor Pridden and Tonya Nelson. 2015. 'Developing 3D Imaging Programmes – Workflow and Quality Control.' *Journal on Computing and Cultural Heritage* 9 (1): 1–11. doi:10.1145/2786760.

Hicks, Dan. 2010. 'The Material-Cultural Turn: Event and Effect.' In *The Oxford Handbook of Material Culture Studies*, edited by Dan Hicks and Mary C. Beaudry, 25–98. Oxford: Oxford University Press.

Hill, Jude. 2006. 'Travelling Objects: The Wellcome Collection in Los Angeles, London and beyond.' *Cultural Geographies* 13 (3): 340–66. doi:10.1191/1474474006eu363oa.

Hinsley, Curtis M., and Bill Holm. 1976. 'A Cannibal in the National Museum: The Early Career of Franz Boas in America.' *American Anthropologist* 78 (2): 306–16.

Hinsley, Curtis M., and David R. Wilcox, eds. 2016. *Coming of Age in Chicago: The 1893 World's Fair and the Coalescence of American Anthropology*. Lincoln: University of Nebraska Press.

Hjorth, Larissa, Heather A. Horst, Anne Galloway and Genevieve Bell, eds. 2017. *The Routledge Companion to Digital Ethnography*. New York: Routledge, Taylor & Francis Group.

Hogsden, Carl, and Emma K. Poulter. 2012. 'The Real Other? Museum Objects in Digital Contact Networks.' *Journal of Material Culture* 17 (3): 265–86. doi:10.1177/1359183512453809.

Holbraad, Martin, and Morten Axel Pedersen. 2017. *The Ontological Turn: An Anthropological Exposition*. Cambridge: Cambridge University Press.

Holbraad, Martin, Morten Axel Pedersen and Eduardo Viveiros de Castro. 2016. 'The Politics of Ontology: Anthropological Positions – Cultural Anthropology.' Available at: https://culanth.org/fieldsights/462-the-politics-of-ontology-anthropological-positions.

Hollinger, R. Eric, John Jr. Edwell, Harold Jacobs, Laura Moran-Collins, Carolyn Thome, Jonathan Zastrow, Adam Metallo, Günter Waibel and Vince Rossi. 2013. 'Tlingit-Smithsonian Collaborations with 3D Digitization of Cultural Objects.' *Museum Anthropology Review* 7 (1–2). Available at: https://scholarworks.iu.edu/journals/index.php/mar/article/view/2173. Last accessed 8 January 2018.

Hooper-Greenhill, Eilean. 1992. *Museums and the Shaping of Knowledge*. London and New York: Routledge.

———. 1994. *Museums and Their Visitors*. London and New York: Routledge.

Horst, Heather A., and Daniel Miller. 2012. *Digital Anthropology*. London and New York: Berg.

Hoskins, Janet. 1998. *Biographical Objects: How Things Tell the Stories of People's Lives*. New York: Routledge.

Howes, Philip, and Zoe Laughlin. 2012. *Material Matters: New Materials in Design*. London: Black Dog Publishing.

Hu, Tung-Hui. 2015. *A Prehistory of the Cloud*. Cambridge, Massachusetts: The MIT Press.

Hui, Yuk. 2012. What Is a Digital Object? *Metaphilosophy* 43 (4): 380–95. doi:10.1111/j.1467-9973.2012.01761.x.

Ingold, Tim. 2007. Materials against Materiality. *Archaeological Dialogues* 14 (1): 1–16. doi:10.1017/S1380203807002127.

———. 2013. *Making: Anthropology, Archaeology, Art and Architecture*. London and New York: Routledge.

Irmscher, Christoph. 1999. *The Poetics of Natural History: From John Bartram to William James*. New Brunswick, N.J.: Rutgers University Press.

Isaac, Gwyneira. 2007. *Mediating Knowledges: Origins of a Zuni Tribal Museum*. Tucson: University of Arizona Press.

———. 2008. 'Technology Becomes the Object: The Use of Electronic Media at the National Museum of the American Indian.' *Journal of Material Culture* 13 (3): 287–310.

———. 2015. 'Perclusive Alliances.' *Current Anthropology* 56 (S12): S286–96. doi:10.1086/683296.

Jacknis, Ira. 1985. 'Franz Boas and Exhibits: On the Limitations of the Museum Method of Anthropology.' In *Objects and Others: Essays on Museums and Material Culture*, edited by George W. Stocking, 75–111. Madison, Wis.: University of Wisconsin Press.

———. 2002. *The Storage Box of Tradition: Kwakiutl Art, Anthropologists, and Museums, 1881–1981*. Washington, D.C.: Smithsonian Institution Press.

———. 2004. 'A Magic Place: The Northwest Coast Indian Hall at the American Museum of Natural History.' In *Coming to Shore: Northwest Coast Ethnology, Traditions and Visions*, edited by Marie Mauze, Michael E. Harkin and Sergei Kan, 221–50. Lincoln, Nebraska: University of Nebraska Press.

———. 2015. 'In the Field/En Plein Air: The Art of Anthropological Display at the American Museum of Natural History, 1905–1930.' In *The Anthropology of Expeditions: Travel, Visualities, Afterlives*, edited by Joshua A. Bell and Erin L. Hasinoff. Cultural Histories of the Material World. New York: Bard Graduate Center.

Jacobs, Karen. 2011. *Collecting Kamoro: Objects, Encounters and Representation in Papua (Western New Guinea)*. Leiden, The Netherlands: Sidestone Press.

Jenkins, David. 1994. 'Object Lessons and Ethnographic Displays: Museum Exhibitions and the Making of American Anthropology.' *Comparative Studies in Society and History* 36 (2): 242–70. doi:10.1017/S0010417500019046.

Johnson, Christopher D. 2012. *Memory, Metaphor and Aby Warburg's Atlas of Images*. Ithaca, New York: Cornell University Press and Cornell University Library.

Kallinikos, Jannis, Aleksi Aaltonen and Attila Marton. 2010. 'A Theory of Digital Objects.' *First Monday* 15 (6–7). Available at: http://www.firstmonday.org/htbin/cgiwrap/bin/ojs/index.php/fm/article/view/3033/2564 (last accessed 8 January 2018).

———. 2013. 'The Ambivalent Ontology of Digital Artifacts.' *MIS Quarterly* 37 (2): 357–70.

Kelty, Christopher M. 2008. *Two Bits: The Cultural Significance of Free Software*. Durham, N.C.; Chesham: Duke University Press; Combined Academic distributor.

Kelty, Christopher, Aaron Panofsky, Morgan Currie, Roderic Crooks, Seth Erickson, Patricia Garcia, Michael Wartenbe and Stacy Wood. 2015. 'Seven Dimensions of Contemporary Participation Disentangled: Seven Dimensions of Contemporary Participation Disentangled.' *Journal of the Association for Information Science and Technology* 66 (3): 474–88. doi:10.1002/asi.23202.

Kenderdine, Sarah. 2016. 'Embodiment, Entanglement and Immersion in Digital Cultural Heritage.' In *A New Companion to Digital Humanities*, edited by Susan Schreibman, Raymond George Siemens and John Unsworth, 22–41. London: John Wiley & Sons.

Keramidas, Kimon. 2015. *The Interface Experience: A User's Guide*. Chicago: University of Chicago Press.

Kirschenbaum, Matthew G. 2012. *Mechanisms: New Media and the Forensic Imagination*. Cambridge, Mass.: MIT Press.

Knox, Hannah, and Antonia Walford. 2016. 'Is There an Ontology to the Digital?' on 'Theorizing the Contemporary', *Cultural Anthropology* website. 24 March. Available at: https://culanth.org/fieldsights/818-is-there-an-ontology-to-the-digital. Last accessed 8 January 2018.

Kopytoff, Igor. 1986. 'The Cultural Biography of Things: Commoditization as Process.' In *The Social Life of Things: Commodities in Cultural Perspective*, edited by Arjun Appadurai, 64–94. Cambridge: Cambridge University Press.

Krmpotich, Cara Ann, and Laura L. Peers. 2013. *This Is Our Life: Haida Material Heritage and Changing Museum Practice*. Vancouver, B.C. and Toronto: UBC Press.

Krmpotich, Cara, Joost Fontein and John Harries. 2010. 'The Substance of Bones: The Emotive Materiality and Affective Presence of Human Remains.' *Journal of Material Culture* 15 (4): 371–84. doi:10.1177/1359183510382965.

Küchler, Susanne. 1987. 'Malangan: Art and Memory in a Melanesian Society.' *Man* 22 (2): 238–55.

———. 1997. 'Sacrificial Economy and Its Objects Rethinking Colonial Collecting in Oceania.' *Journal of Material Culture* 2 (1): 39–60. doi:10.1177/135918359700200102.

———. 2002. *Malanggan: Art, Memory and Sacrifice*. Oxford and New York: Berg 3PL.

———. 2013. 'Barkcloth and Odour.' In *Properties and Social Imagination*, edited by Adam Drazin, Haidy Geismar and Camilla Sundwall, 42–3. UCL Anthropology: Material World Occasional Paper 4.

Lamb, Jonathan. 2011. *The Things Things Say*. Princeton: Princeton University Press.

Larkin, Brian. 2013. 'The Politics and Poetics of Infrastructure.' *Annual Review of Anthropology* 42 (1): 327–43. doi:10.1146/annurev-anthro-092412-155522.

Latour, Bruno. 1993. *We Have Never Been Modern*. Cambridge, Mass.: Harvard University Press.

Laurenson, Pip, Vivian Van Saaze and O. Remes. 2014. 'Collecting Performance-Based Art: New Challenges and Shifting Perspectives.' In *Performativity in the Gallery: Staging Interactive Encounters*, 27–41. Bern: Pater Lang.

Lemonnier, Pierre. 2012. *Mundane Objects: Materiality and Non-Verbal Communication*. Abingdon: Left Coast Press.

Leonardi, Paul M. 2010. 'Digital Materiality? How Artifacts without Matter, Matter.' *First Monday* 15 (6). Available at: http://firstmonday.org/ojs/index.php/fm/article/view/3036. Last accessed 8 January 2018.

Lessig, Lawrence. 2006. *Code: Version 2.0*. 2nd ed. New York: Basic Books.

Lonetree, Amy. 2012. *Decolonizing Museums: Representing Native America in National and Tribal Museums*. Chapel Hill, N.C.: UNC Press Books.

Lynes, Russell. 1981. *More than Meets the Eye: The History and Collections of the Cooper-Hewitt Museum*. Washington, D.C.: Smithsonian Institution.

MacDonald, Sally, Mona Hess, Stuart Robson and Graeme Were. 2012. '3D Recording and Museums.' In *Digital Humanities in Practice*, edited by Claire Warwick, Melissa M. Terras and Julianne Nyhan, 91–115. London: Facet Publishing in association with UCL Centre for Digital Humanities.

Macdonald, Sharon. 2015. 'The Trouble with the Ethnological.' In *The Laboratory Concept. Museum Experiments in the Humboldt Lab Dahlem*, 211–28. Berlin: Nicolaische Verlagsbuchd.

———. 2016. 'New Constellations of Difference in Europe's 21st-Century Museumscape.' *Museum Anthropology* 39 (1): 4–19. doi:10.1111/muan.12104.

MacGregor, Neil. 2012. *A History of the World in 100 Objects*. London and New York, Toronto: Penguin Books.

MacKenzie, Maureen Anne. 1991. *Androgynous Objects: String Bags and Gender in Central New Guinea*. Chur, Switzerland, Philadelphia: Harwood Academic Publishers.

Malraux, André. 1967. *Museum without Walls*. London: Secker & Warburg.

Manovich, Lev. 2013. *Software Takes Command: Extending the Language of New Media*. International Texts in Critical Media Aesthetics. London: Bloomsbury Publishing.

Marres, Noortje. 2012. *Material Participation: Technology, the Environment and Everyday Publics*. Houndmills, Basingstoke, Hampshire and New York: Palgrave Macmillan.

Mauss, Marcel. 2006. *Techniques, Technology and Civilisation*. Oxford: Berghahn.

McCarty, Cara. 2014. 'Introduction.' In *Making Design*, 27–31. New York: Cooper Hewitt, Smithsonian Design Museum.

Mead, Sidney Moko. 1990. 'The Nature of Taonga. Paper Presented and Published within Taonga Māori Conference.' Wellington, Aotearoa/New Zealand: Department of Internal Affairs/Te Tari Taiwhenua.

———. 2003. *Tikanga Māori: Living by Māori Values*. Wellington: Huia Publishers.

Metge, Joan. 2010. 'Huara Ngātia: Māori Words in New Zealand English.' In *Tuamaka: The Challenge of Difference in Aotearoa New Zealand*, Joan Metge, 55–107. Auckland, N.Z.: Auckland University Press.

Michaud, Philippe-Alain. 2004. *Aby Warburg and the Image in Motion*. New York: Zone Books.

Miller, Daniel. 1987. *Material Culture and Mass Consumption*. Oxford: Blackwell.

———. 2005. 'Materiality: An Introduction.' In *Materiality*, edited by Daniel Miller, 1–50. Durham, N.C.: Duke University Press.

———. 2010. 'Anthropology in Blue Jeans.' *American Ethnologist* 37 (3): 415–28. doi:10.1111/j.1548-1425.2010.01263.x.

Miller, Daniel, and Christopher Tilley. 1996. 'Editorial.' *Journal of Material Culture* 1 (1): 5–14. doi:10.1177/135918359600100101.

Mintz, Sidney Wilfred. 1986. *Sweetness and Power: The Place of Sugar in Modern History*. New York: Penguin Books.

Miodownik, Mark. 2013. *Stuff Matters: The Strange Stories of the Marvellous Materials That Shape Our Man-Made World*. New York: Viking.

———. 2015. 'Towards Designing New Sensoaesthetic Materials: The Role of Materials Libraries.' In *The Social Life of* Material, edited by Adam Drazin and Susanne Küchler, 69–80. London and New York: Bloomsbury Academic.

Mitchell, W.J.T. 1996. 'What Do Pictures "Really" Want?' *October* 77 (July): 71–82. doi:10.2307/778960.

———. 2002. 'Showing Seeing: A Critique of Visual Culture.' *Journal of Visual Culture* 1 (2): 165–81. doi:10.1177/147041290200100202.

———. 2005. 'There Are No Visual Media.' *Journal of Visual Culture* 4 (2): 257–66. doi:10.1177/1470412905054673.

Mithlo, Nancy Marie. 2004. 'Red Man's Burden: The Politics of Inclusion in Museum Settings.' *American Indian Quarterly* 28 (3/4): 743–63.

Morozov, Evgeny. 2012. *The Net Delusion: The Dark Side of Internet Freedom*. Reprint ed. New York: PublicAffairs.

Moutu, Andrew. 2007. 'Collection as a Way of Being.' In *Thinking Through Things: Theorising Artefacts Ethnographically*, edited by Amiria Henare, Martin Holbraad and Sari Wastell, 93–112. London and New York: Routledge.

Nardi, Bonnie. 2015. 'Virtuality.' *Annual Review of Anthropology* 44 (1): 15–31. doi:10.1146/annurev-anthro-102214-014226.

Newitz, Annalee. 2016. 'One of the Greatest Art Heists of Our Time Was Actually a Data Hack.' Ars Technica UK. 11 March 2016. Available at: https://arstechnica.co.uk/tech-policy/2016/03/one-of-the-greatest-art-heists-of-our-time-was-actually-a-data-hack/. Last accessed 8 January 2018

Ngata, Wayne, Hera Ngata-Gibson and Amiria Salmond. 2012. 'Te Ataakura: Digital Taonga and Cultural Innovation.' *Journal of Material Culture* 17 (3): 229–44. doi:10.1177/1359183512453807.

O'Hanlon, Michael. 2014. *The Pitt Rivers Museum*. London and Boston: Scala Arts and Heritage Publishers Ltd and Pitt Rivers Museum.

O'Hanlon, Michael, and Robert Louis Welsch. 2000. *Hunting the Gatherers : Ethnographic Collectors, Agents and Agency in Melanesia, 1870s–1930s*. New York: Berghahn Books.

Parkin, Robert. 2009. 'Oxford Anthropology as an Extra-Curriular Activity: OUAS and JASO.' In *A History of Oxford Anthropology*, edited by Peter Riviere, 137–54. Oxford: Berghahn Books.

Parry, Ross. 2013. 'The End of the Beginning: Normativity in the Postdigital Museum.' *Museum Worlds: Advances in Research* 1: 24–39.

Pearce, Susan M. 1990. *Objects of Knowledge*. London: Athlone Press.

Peers, Laura L., and Alison K. Brown. 2003. *Museums and Source Communities: A Routledge Reader*. London and New York: Routledge.

Phillips, Ruth. 2011. 'The Digital R/Evolution of Museum-Based Research.' In *Museum Pieces: Essays on the Indigenization of Canadian Museums*, Ruth B. Phillips. Kingston: McGill University Press.

Pink, Sarah, Elisenda Ardèvol and Dèbora Lanzeni, eds. 2016. *Digital Materialities: Design and Anthropology*. London and New York: Bloomsbury Academic.

Pinney, Christopher. 2008. 'The Prosthetic Eye: Photography as Cure and Poison.' *Journal of the Royal Anthropological Institute* 14 (April): S33–46. doi:10.1111/j.1467-9655.2008.00491.x.

Poignant, Roslyn. 2004. *Professional Savages : Captive Lives and Western Spectacle*. New Haven: Yale University Press.

Povinelli, Elizabeth A. 2011. 'The Woman on the Other Side of the Wall: Archiving the Otherwise in Postcolonial Digital Archives.' *Differences* 22 (1): 146–71. doi:10.1215/10407391-1218274.

Pratt, Mary Louise. 1991. 'Arts of the Contact Zone.' *Profession*, 33–40.

Price, Sally. 2007. *Paris Primitive: Jacques Chirac's Museum on the Quai Branly*. Chicago: University of Chicago Press.

Quinn, Stephen Christopher. 2006. *Windows on Nature*. New York: Harry N. Abrams.

Rader, Karen A., and Victoria E. Cain. 2014. *Life on Display: Revolutionizing US Museums of Science and Natural History in the Twentieth Century*. Chicago: University of Chicago Press.

Raymond, Rosanna. 2003. 'Getting Specific: Pacific Fashion Activism in Auckland during the 1990s.' In *Clothing the Pacific*, edited by Chloë Colchester, 193–208. Oxford: Berg.

Raymond, Rosanna, and Amiria Manutahi Salmond. 2008. *Pasifika Styles: Artists inside the Museum*. Cambridge: University of Cambridge Museum of Archaeology and Anthropology, in association with Otago University Press.

Renshaw, Layla. 2010. 'The Scientific and Affective Identification of Republican Civilian Victims from the Spanish Civil War.' *Journal of Material Culture* 15 (4): 449–63. doi:10.1177/1359183510382961.

Rheingold, Howard. 2003. *Smart Mobs: The Next Social Revolution*. Cambridge, Mass.: Basic Books.

Rickard, Jolene. 2007. 'Absorbing or Obscuring the Absence of a Critical Space in the Americas for Indigeneity: The Smithsonian's National Museum of the American Indian.' *Res: Anthropology and Aesthetics* 52 (Fall): 56–74.

Rio, Knut M. 2002. 'The Third Man: Manifestations of Agency on Ambrym Island, Vanuatu.' Dissertation for DrPolit degree, Department of Social Anthropology, University of Bergen.

Robb, John. 2015. 'What Do Things Want? Object Design as a Middle Range Theory of Material Culture: Object Design as a Middle Range Theory of Material Culture.' *Archeological Papers of the American Anthropological Association* 26 (1): 166–80. doi:10.1111/apaa.12069.

Rowley, Susan. 2013. 'The Reciprocal Research Network: The Development Process.' *Museum Anthropology Review* 7 (1–2): 22–43.

Ruskin, John. 2003 [1853]. *The Stones of Venice*. New York: DaCapo Press.

———. 1868. *The Political Economy of Art*. London: Smith, Elder & Company.

Russell, Georgina. 1987. 'The Wellcome Historical Medical Museum's Dispersal of Non-Medical Material, 1936 to 1983.' *Newsletter (Museum Ethnographers Group)*, 20: 21–45.

Said, Edward W. 2003. *Orientalism*. 25th anniversary ed. with 1995 afterword ed. London: Penguin Books.

Salmond, Amiria Manutahi. 2013. 'Transforming Translations (Part I): "The Owner of These Bones."' *HAU: Journal of Ethnographic Theory* 3 (3): 1–32. doi:10.14318/hau3.3.001.

Salmond, Anne. 1997. *Between Worlds: Early Exchanges between Māori and Europeans, 1773–1815*. Honolulu: University of Hawai'i Press.

Scholze, Jana. 2016. 'Ghosts and Dancers: Immaterials and the Museum.' In *Design Objects and the Museum*, edited by Liz Farrelly and Joanna Weddell, 61–72. London: Bloomsbury Publishing.

Schorch, Philipp, and Arapata Hakiwai. 2014. 'Mana Taonga and the Public Sphere: A Dialogue between Indigenous Practice and Western Theory.' *International Journal of Cultural Studies* 17 (2): 191–205. doi:10.1177/1367877913482785.

Shep, Sydney J. 2016. 'Digital Materiality.' In *A New Companion to Digital Humanities*, edited by Susan Schreibman, Raymond George Siemens and John Unsworth, 322–30. Oxford: John Wiley & Sons.

Shirky, Clay. 2009. *Here Comes Everybody: How Change Happens When People Come Together*. London: Penguin.

Smith, Huhana. 2008. 'Hei Wai Ora: A Photo Essay.' *International Journal of Cultural Property* 15 (2). doi:10.1017/S0940739108080119.

Smith, Paul Chaat. 2009. *Everything You Know about Indians Is Wrong*. Minneapolis, Minn. and London: University of Minnesota Press.

Speiser, Felix. 1996. *Ethnology of Vanuatu: An Early Twentieth Century Study*. Translated by D.Q. Stephenson. University of Hawai'i Press.

Srinivasan, Ramesh, Robin Boast, Jonathan Furner and Katherine M. Becvar. 2009. 'Digital Museums and Diverse Cultural Knowledges: Moving Past the Traditional Catalog.' *The Information Society* 25 (4): 265–78.

Stanley, Nick. 1998. *Being Ourselves for You: The Global Display of Cultures*. London: Middlesex University Press.

———. 2012. *The Making of Asmat Art: Indigenous Art in a World Perspective*. Canon Pyon: Sean Kingston.

Star, Susan Leigh. 1999. 'The Ethnography of Infrastructure.' *American Behavioral Scientist* 43 (3): 377–91. doi:10.1177/00027649921955326.

Starosielski, Nicole. 2015. *The Undersea Network*. Durham, N.C.: Duke University Press Books.

Sterne, Jonathan. 2012. *MP3: The Meaning of a Format*. Durham, N.C.: Duke University Press Books.

Steyerl, Hito. 2009. 'In Defense of the Poor Image.' Journal #10, November, *e-flux*. http://www.e-flux.com/journal/10/61362/in-defense-of-the-poor-image/. (last accessed 8 January 2018).

Stocking, George W. 1985. *Objects and Others: Essays on Museums and Material Culture*. Madison: University of Wisconsin Press.

Tapsell, Paul. 1997. 'The Flight of Pareraututu: An Investigation of Taonga from a Tribal Perspective.' *Journal of the Polynesian Society* 106 (4): 323–74.

———. 2000. *Pukaki: A Comet Returns*. Auckland: Reed Publishing.

———. 2006. 'Taonga, Marae, Whenua – Negotiating Custodianship: A Maori Tribal Response to Te Papa: The Museum of New Zealand.' In *Rethinking Settler Colonialism: History and Memory in Australia, Canada, Aotearoa New Zealand and South Africa*, Annie E. Coombes, 86–99. Studies in Imperialism. Manchester and New York: Manchester University Press.

———. 2011. 'Aroha Mai: Whose Museum?' In *The Routledge Companion to Museum Ethics: Redefining Ethics for the Twenty-First-Century Museum*, edited by Janet Marstine, 85–111. London: Routledge.

———. 2017. 'Being Pre-Indigenous: Kin Accountability beyond Tradition.' In *The Routledge Companion to Cultural Property*, edited by Jane Anderson and Haidy Geismar, 351–72. London and New York, NY: Routledge.

Taussig, Michael T. 1993. *Mimesis and Alterity: A Particular History of the Senses*. New York: Routledge.

Taylor, J., and Nick Thieberger. 2011. *Working Together in Vanuatu: Research Histories, Collaborations, Projects and Reflections*. Acton, A.C.T.: ANU E Press.

Thomas, Nicholas. 1999. *Possessions: Indigenous Art/Colonial Culture*. New York and London: Thames & Hudson.

Thompson, E.P., and Peter Linebaugh. 2011. *William Morris: Romantic to Revolutionary*. Oakland, C.A.: PM Press.

Tilley, Christopher. 1999. *Metaphor and Material Culture*. Oxford: John Wiley & Sons, Ltd.

Trask, Jeffrey. 2006. '"American Things:" The Cultural Value of Decorative Arts in the Modern Museum, 1905–1931.' Phd, New York: Columbia University.

———. 2013. *Things American: Art Museums and Civic Culture in the Progressive Era*. Philadelphia: University of Pennsylvania Press.

Tsing, Anna Lowenhaupt. 2015. *The Mushroom at the End of the World: On the Possibility of Life in Capitalist Ruins*. Princeton: Princeton University Press.

Turkle, Sherry. 2012. *Alone Together: Why We Expect More from Technology and Less from Each Other*. New York: Basic Books.

Tylor, Edward B. 1881. 'President's Address.' *The Journal of the Anthropological Institute of Great Britain and Ireland* 10: 440–58. Available at: http://www.jstor.org/stable/2841548. (last accessed 8 January 2018).

UCL. 2008. 'AHRC Ethnographic Documentation Project Report.' Unpublished. On file in the UCL Ethnography Collections in the UCL Department of Anthropology.

Vergo, Peter. 1989. *The New Museology*. London: Reaktion Books.

Verran, Helen, and Michael Christie. 2014. 'Postcolonial Databasing? Subverting Old Appropriations, Developing New Associations.' In *Subversion, Conversion, Development: Cross-Cultural Knowledge Exchange and the Politics of Design*, edited by James Leach and Lee Wilson, 57–78. Cambridge, Mass.: MIT Press.

Veys, Fanny Wonu. 2017. *Unwrapping Tongan Barkcloth: Encounters, Creativity and Female Agency*. London and New York: Bloomsbury.

Viveiros de Castro, Eduardo. 1998. 'Cosmological Deixis and Amerindian Perspectivism.' *The Journal of the Royal Anthropological Institute* 4 (3):469–88. doi:10.2307/3034157.

Vizenor, Gerald. 2011. *Literary Chance: Essays on Native American Survivance*. Universitat de València.

Wang, Shu Li, and Michael Rowlands. 2017. 'Making and Unmaking Heritage Values in China.' In *The Routledge Companion to Cultural Property*, edited by Jane Anderson and Haidy Geismar, 258–76. Abingdon, Oxon and New York, NY: Routledge.

Webster, Gloria Cranmer. 1990. 'The U'mista Cultural Centre.' *The Massachusetts Review* 31 (1/2): 132–43.

Were, Graeme. 2013. 'On the Materials of Mats: Thinking through Design in a Melanesian Society: On the Materials of Mats.' *Journal of the Royal Anthropological Institute* 19 (3): 581–99. doi:10.1111/1467-9655.12051.

———. 2014. 'Digital Heritage, Knowledge Networks, and Source Communities: Understanding Digital Objects in a Melanesian Society.' *Museum Anthropology* 37 (2): 133–43. doi:10.1111/muan.12058.

Were, Graeme, and J.C.H. King, eds. 2012. *Extreme Collecting: Challenging Practices for 21st Century Museums*. New York: Berghahn Books.

Werner, Paul. 2005. *Museum, Inc.: Inside the Global Art World*. Chicago, Ill: Prickly Paradigm Press.

Weschler, Lawrence. 1997. *Mr Wilson's Cabinet of Wonder*. New York: Vintage Books.

Wilder, Charley. 2016a. 'Swiping a priceless antiquity … with a scanner and a 3D printer.' *The New York Times*: Art and Design section. 1 March 2016. Available at: https://www.nytimes.com/2016/03/02/arts/design/other-nefertiti-3d-printer.html?_r=0. (last accessed 8 January 2018).

———. 2016b. 'Nefertiti 3-D scanning project in Germany raises doubts.' *The New York Times*: Art and Design section. 10 March 2016. https://www.nytimes.com/2016/03/11/arts/design/nefertiti-3-d-scanning-project-in-germany-raises-doubts.html. (last accessed 8 January 2018).

Wilkes, Sarah Elizabeth. 2011. 'Materials Libraries as Vehicles for Knowledge Transfer.' *Knowledge Transfer: Exchanging Knowledge with the Field, Anthropology Matters* 13 (1). Available at: https://www.anthropologymatters.com/index.php/anth_matters/article/view/233/413. (last accessed 8 January 2018).

Williams, Paul Harvey. 2007. *Memorial Museums: The Global Rush to Commemorate Atrocities*. Oxford and New York: Berg.

Wilson, Cody. 2016. *Come and Take It: The Gun Printer's Guide to Thinking Free*. New York: Gallery Books.

Wilson, Ross J. 2011. 'Behind the Scenes of the Museum Website.' *Museum Management and Curatorship* 26 (4): 373–89. doi:10.1080/09647775.2011.603934.

Zorach, Rebecca, and Elizabeth Rodini. 2005. *Paper Museums: The Reproductive Print in Europe, 1500–1800*. Chicago, Ill: David and Alfred Smart Museum of Art, University of Chicago.

Index

CPSIA information can be obtained
at www.ICGtesting.com
Printed in the USA
BVHW06s1103160918
527476BV00023BA/270/P

9 781787 352827